Intensive Listening Training

David Bohlke • Anne Taylor

Intensive Listening Training 3

David Bohlke • Anne Taylor

7212 Canary Lane,
Sachse, TX, USA

Acquisitions Editor: Rose Morgan
Content Editor: Liana Robinson
Copy Editor: Tracey Blash
Cover/Design: Highline Studio

http://www.seed-learning.com

ISBN: 978-1-9464-5293-1

10 9 8 7 6 5 4 3 2
22 21 20 19 18

Photo Credits

Contents

How to Use This Book

Intensive Listening Training is a three-book series designed to develop the aural comprehension skills of English language learners at the high-beginning to intermediate level. Units within the series focus on typical speech routines thematically categorized into situational topics. Listening tasks in each unit range from testing discrete listening items to checking general comprehension of short dialogs and talks to completing dictation pages. Each level in the *Intensive Listening Training* series includes more than 180 minutes of audio input for learners to use for practice as they hone their English aural skills.

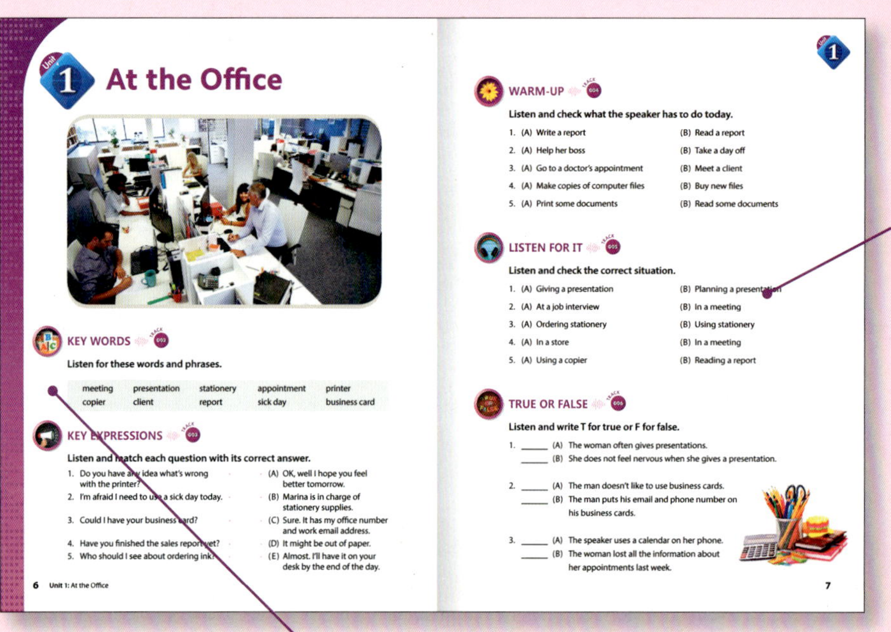

Unit 1 At the Office

KEY WORDS

Listen for these words and phrases.

meeting · presentation · stationery · appointment · printer · copier · client · report · sick day · business card

KEY EXPRESSIONS

Listen and match each question with its correct answer.

1. Do you have any idea what's wrong with the printer?
2. I'm afraid I need to use a sick day today.
3. Could I have your business card?
4. Have you finished the sales report yet?
5. Who should I see about ordering ink?

(A) OK, well I hope you feel better tomorrow.
(B) Marina is in charge of stationery supplies.
(C) Sure. It has my office number and work email address.
(D) It might be out of paper.
(E) Almost. I'll have it on your desk by the end of the day.

6 Unit 1: At the Office

WARM-UP

Listen and check what the speaker has to do today.

1. (A) Write a report (B) Read a report
2. (A) Help her boss (B) Take a day off
3. (A) Go to a doctor's appointment (B) Meet a client
4. (A) Make copies of computer files (B) Buy new files
5. (A) Print some documents (B) Read some documents

LISTEN FOR IT

Listen and check the correct situation.

1. (A) Giving a presentation (B) Planning a presentation
2. (A) At a job interview (B) In a meeting
3. (A) Ordering stationery (B) Using stationery
4. (A) In a store (B) In a meeting
5. (A) Using a copier (B) Reading a report

TRUE OR FALSE

Listen and write T for true or F for false.

1. ____ (A) The woman often gives presentations.
   ____ (B) She does not feel nervous when she gives a presentation.
2. ____ (A) The man doesn't like to use business cards.
   ____ (B) The man puts his email and phone number on his business cards.
3. ____ (A) The speaker uses a calendar on her phone.
   ____ (B) The woman lost all the information about her appointments last week.

7

WARM-UP, LISTEN FOR IT, & TRUE OR FALSE

These three activities provide listening practice, progressing from discreet listening at the sentence level in **WARM-UP** and **LISTEN FOR IT** to general comprehension in the short talks in **TRUE OR FALSE**.

KEY WORDS & KEY EXPRESSIONS

The first page in each themed unit introduces useful vocabulary and expressions which the students will hear in the various activities throughout the unit. In **KEY EXPRESSIONS**, students match a question with the best response.

For additional practice, have students check their answers in pairs by role-playing the question-answer dialogs before listening for the answers.

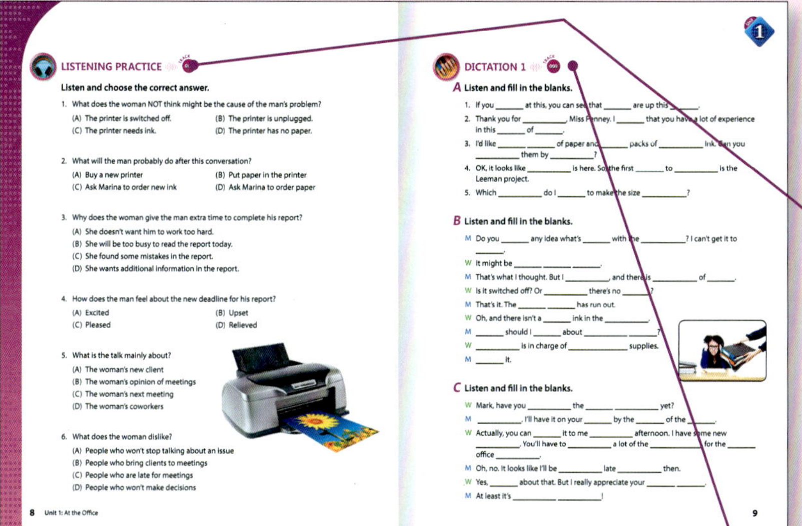

LISTENING PRACTICE

In **LISTENING PRACTICE**, students will answer comprehension questions about a variety of dialogs and short talks.

For additional practice, students can read the transcripts and highlight the key words and expressions from the first page of the unit.

DICTATION 1

In **DICTATION 1**, students revisit some of the dialogs and talks from the previous sections and practice listening for discrete items. Students will listen for individual words and check their ability to recognize sounds and spell them correctly.

Students can compare their answers with a partner, then check the answers as a class. Students working alone should check the transcripts at the back of the book.

LISTENING TEST

The dialogs and talks in **LISTENING TEST** build on the language introduced in the previous activities.

For additional practice, have students work in pairs to create their own dialogs based on the transcripts.

DICTATION 2

As in **DICTATION 1**, students will listen for individual words and check their ability to recognize sounds and spell them correctly.

For additional practice, students can work in pairs and read the transcript together. This will allow students to practice their reading and pronunciation skills in addition to listening and writing.

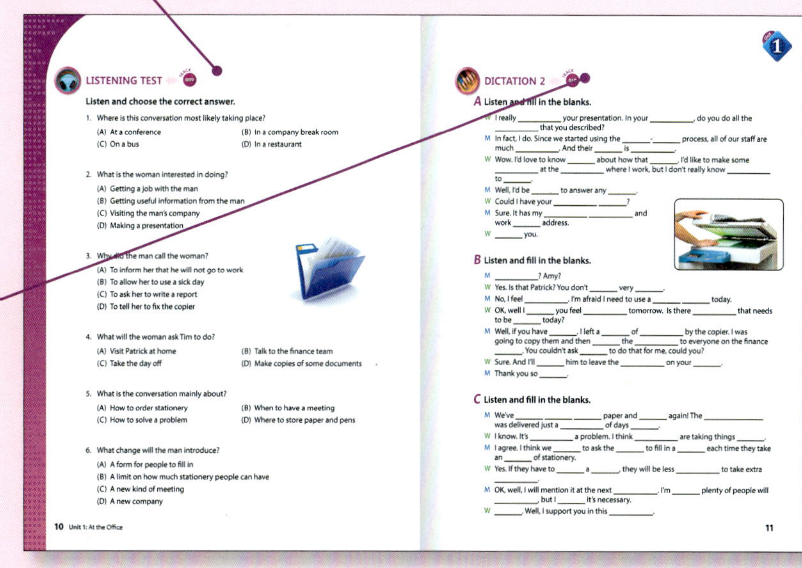

At the Office

KEY WORDS

Listen for these words and phrases.

meeting	presentation	stationery	appointment	printer
copier	client	report	sick day	business card

KEY EXPRESSIONS

Listen and match each question with its correct answer.

1. Do you have any idea what's wrong with the printer?
2. I'm afraid I need to use a sick day today.
3. Could I have your business card?
4. Have you finished the sales report yet?
5. Who should I see about ordering ink?

(A) OK, well I hope you feel better tomorrow.
(B) Marina is in charge of stationery supplies.
(C) Sure. It has my office number and work email address.
(D) It might be out of paper.
(E) Almost. I'll have it on your desk by the end of the day.

WARM-UP

TRACK 004

Listen and check what the speaker has to do today.

1. (A) Write a report (B) Read a report
2. (A) Help her boss (B) Take a day off
3. (A) Go to a doctor's appointment (B) Meet a client
4. (A) Make copies of computer files (B) Buy new files
5. (A) Print some documents (B) Read some documents

LISTEN FOR IT

TRACK 005

Listen and check the correct situation.

1. (A) Giving a presentation (B) Planning a presentation
2. (A) At a job interview (B) In a meeting
3. (A) Ordering stationery (B) Using stationery
4. (A) In a store (B) In a meeting
5. (A) Using a copier (B) Reading a report

TRUE OR FALSE

TRACK 006

Listen and write T for true or F for false.

1. _______ (A) The woman often gives presentations.
   _______ (B) She does not feel nervous when she gives a presentation.

2. _______ (A) The man doesn't like to use business cards.
   _______ (B) The man puts his email and phone number on his business cards.

3. _______ (A) The speaker uses a calendar on her phone.
   _______ (B) The woman lost all the information about her appointments last week.

LISTENING PRACTICE

Listen and choose the correct answer.

1. What does the woman NOT think might be the cause of the man's problem?
   (A) The printer is switched off.
   (B) The printer is unplugged.
   (C) The printer needs ink.
   (D) The printer has no paper.

2. What will the man probably do after this conversation?
   (A) Buy a new printer
   (B) Put paper in the printer
   (C) Ask Marina to order new ink
   (D) Ask Marina to order paper

3. Why does the woman give the man extra time to complete his report?
   (A) She doesn't want him to work too hard.
   (B) She will be too busy to read the report today.
   (C) She found some mistakes in the report.
   (D) She wants additional information in the report.

4. How does the man feel about the new deadline for his report?
   (A) Excited
   (B) Upset
   (C) Pleased
   (D) Relieved

5. What is the talk mainly about?
   (A) The woman's new client
   (B) The woman's opinion of meetings
   (C) The woman's next meeting
   (D) The woman's coworkers

6. What does the woman dislike?
   (A) People who won't stop talking about an issue
   (B) People who bring clients to meetings
   (C) People who are late for meetings
   (D) People who won't make decisions

DICTATION 1

A Listen and fill in the blanks.

1. If you _______ at this, you can see that _______ are up this _______.
2. Thank you for ___________, Miss Penney. I _______ that you have a lot of experience in this _______ of _______.
3. I'd like _______ _______ of paper and _______ packs of ___________ ink. Can you ___________ them by ___________?
4. OK, it looks like ___________ is here. So, the first _______ to ___________ is the Leeman project.
5. Which ___________ do I _______ to make the size ___________?

B Listen and fill in the blanks.

M Do you _______ any idea what's _______ with the ___________? I can't get it to _______.

W It might be _______ _______ _______.

M That's what I thought. But I ___________, and there is ___________ of _______.

W Is it switched off? Or ___________ there's no _______?

M That's it. The _______ _______ has run out.

W Oh, and there isn't a _______ ink in the ___________.

M _______ should I _______ about ___________ _______?

W ___________ is in charge of _______________ supplies.

M _______ it.

C Listen and fill in the blanks.

W Mark, have you ___________ the _______ ___________ yet?

M ___________. I'll have it on your _______ by the _______ of the _______.

W Actually, you can _______ it to me ___________ afternoon. I have some new ___________. You'll have to ___________ a lot of the _____________ for the _______ office ___________.

M Oh, no. It looks like I'll be ___________ late ___________ then.

W Yes, _______ about that. But I really appreciate your _______ _______.

M At least it's ___________ ___________!

LISTENING TEST

Listen and choose the correct answer.

1. Where is this conversation most likely taking place?
   (A) At a conference
   (B) In a company break room
   (C) On a bus
   (D) In a restaurant

2. What is the woman interested in doing?
   (A) Getting a job with the man
   (B) Getting useful information from the man
   (C) Visiting the man's company
   (D) Making a presentation

3. Why did the man call the woman?
   (A) To inform her that he will not go to work
   (B) To allow her to use a sick day
   (C) To ask her to write a report
   (D) To tell her to fix the copier

4. What will the woman ask Tim to do?
   (A) Visit Patrick at home
   (B) Talk to the finance team
   (C) Take the day off
   (D) Make copies of some documents

5. What is this conversation mainly about?
   (A) How to order stationery
   (B) When to have a meeting
   (C) How to solve a problem
   (D) Where to store paper and pens

6. What change will the man introduce?
   (A) A form for people to fill in
   (B) A limit on how much stationery people can have
   (C) A new kind of meeting
   (D) A new company

DICTATION 2

A Listen and fill in the blanks.

W I really ________ your presentation. In your ________________, do you do all the ____________ that you described?

M In fact, I do. Since we started using the ________-________ process, all of our staff are much ____________. And their ________ is ____________.

W Wow. I'd love to know ________ about how that ________. I'd like to make some ____________ at the ____________ where I work, but I don't really know ________ to ________.

M Well, I'd be ________ to answer any ____________.

W Could I have your ____________ ________?

M Sure. It has my ____________ ____________ and work ________ address.

W ________ you.

B Listen and fill in the blanks.

M ____________? Amy?

W Yes. Is that Patrick? You don't ________ very ________.

M No, I feel ____________. I'm afraid I need to use a ________ ________ today.

W OK, well I ________ you feel ____________ tomorrow. Is there ____________ that needs to be ________ today?

M Well, if you have ________. I left a ________ of ____________ by the copier. I was going to copy them and then ________ the ____________ to everyone on the finance ________. You couldn't ask ________ to do that for me, could you?

W Sure. And I'll ________ him to leave the ____________ on your ________.

M Thank you so ________.

C Listen and fill in the blanks.

M We've ________ ________ ________ paper and ________ again! The ________________ was delivered just a ____________ of days ________.

W I know. It's ____________ a problem. I think ____________ are taking things ________.

M I agree. I think we ________ to ask the ________ to fill in a ________ each time they take an ________ of stationery.

W Yes. If they have to ________ a ________, they will be less ____________ to take extra ____________.

M OK, well, I will mention it at the next ____________. I'm ________ plenty of people will ____________, but I ________ it's necessary.

W ________. Well, I support you in this ____________.

On Time

KEY WORDS

Listen for these words and phrases.

calendar	month	anniversary	schedule	ago
ahead of time	postpone	later	while	promptly

KEY EXPRESSIONS

Listen and match each question with its correct answer.

1. Look at the time. It's already a quarter to one.
2. Is the bus often late?
3. How much longer until we land in Singapore?
4. Has the 3:00 bus already come?
5. What time do you begin work?

(A) About six and a half hours.
(B) I start work at 9:30 every morning.
(C) No, it's usually on time.
(D) Really? How time flies!
(E) Not yet. I've been waiting here since 2:45.

WARM-UP

Listen and check what times the business is open.

1. (A) 8:00 a.m. – 6:00 p.m. (B) 8:30 a.m. – 6:00 p.m.
2. (A) 7:30 a.m. – 11:00 a.m. (B) 6:30 a.m. – 11:00 p.m.
3. (A) 9: 00 a.m. – 12:00 p.m. Saturdays (B) 9:00 a.m. – 6:00 p.m. Saturdays
4. (A) 6:30 a.m. – 8:00 p.m. (B) 6:00 a.m. – 8:30 p.m.
5. (A) 10:00 a.m. – 3:00 p.m. (B) 10:00 a.m. – 5:00 p.m.

LISTEN FOR IT

Listen and check where the speaker has to be at a certain time.

1. (A) At school at 8:05 (B) At the bus stop at 8:05
2. (A) At the train station at 11:45 (B) At Baker Street at 11:45
3. (A) At home by 3:30 p.m. (B) At her parents' house by 3:30 p.m.
4. (A) At an office at 10:40 (B) At an office at 11:00
5. (A) At home by 5:00 p.m. (B) At school by 5:00 p.m.

TRUE OR FALSE

Listen and write T for true or F for false.

1. _______ (A) The woman is going to see a movie with a friend.
   _______ (B) The woman already knows which movie they will watch.

2. _______ (A) The bus will take 20 minutes to reach the airport.
   _______ (B) The driver will collect tickets after the bus arrives at its destination.

3. _______ (A) There will be a talk from 8:30 to 9:45.
   _______ (B) Hot drinks are not allowed in the rooms.

LISTENING PRACTICE

Listen and choose the correct answer.

1. How long have the speakers been at the restaurant?
   (A) A few minutes
   (B) 15 minutes
   (C) 30 minutes
   (D) 45 minutes

2. Which of the following is NOT true about the man's lunch?
   (A) He ordered spaghetti.
   (B) He has not finished eating.
   (C) He enjoyed his food.
   (D) He will leave most of his lunch.

3. What does the woman tell the man to do?
   (A) Take a nap
   (B) Read a schedule
   (C) Read a book
   (D) Listen to music

4. What happened the last time the woman traveled by airplane?
   (A) The flight was early.
   (B) The airplane was very dirty.
   (C) The airplane left very late.
   (D) The flight was canceled.

5. What is this conversation about?
   (A) A late bus
   (B) How often the bus comes
   (C) A dangerous bus driver
   (D) Where to catch the bus

6. Which of the following is true about the bus?
   (A) The three o'clock bus already left.
   (B) The three o'clock bus is not often late.
   (C) There is no bus at four o'clock.
   (D) The bus comes once an hour.

A Listen and fill in the blanks.

1. _______ starts at 9:00, but it takes _____ _______ to get there by _____. I need to be at the _____ _____ at 8:05 if I want to get to _______ on _____.
2. According to the _____ _______, the last _____ to Baker Street _______ at _____. It's already 11:35, so I'll have to _____!
3. It's my _______ 20th _______ anniversary. I have to be at their _____ by 3:30 to _______ their _____ for a _______ _____!
4. I have an __________ for an _______ job at _____. I have to arrive _____ minutes before the _____ of the interview.
5. My mom _______ at me for coming home _____ after _______ last _____, so I have to be _____ by 5:00 _____ _____ from now on.

B Listen and fill in the blanks.

M _____ at the _____! It's already a _______ to one.

W Really? How _____ _____. It's almost _____ to get back to the _______. Why does _____ time always _____ _____ so _______?

M I know. I'd better _____ and _______ my _____. I think I'll get a doggy _____ for the _____ of this spaghetti. It's too _____ to _____.

W We got here at _____, but it seems like only a _____ _______.

M I _____. Let's _____ the _______ and get the _____.

W _____ your _______ away. It's my _____. It is your _______ after all!

C Listen and fill in the blanks.

M How _____ _______ until we _____ in Singapore?

W About _____ and a _____ hours.

M That's _____ so long. I'm getting _____ now.

W You'll just have to _____ your book or _____ another _____. I'm going to try to get some _____. And _______, the _____ said that we will _______ _____ of schedule.

M I guess that's a _____ _____.

W Well, it's a lot _______ than arriving behind schedule. _____ _____ I traveled by _______, we left _____ _____ late!

Listen and choose the correct answer.

1. What hours does the woman usually work?
   (A) From 10:00 to 6:00
   (B) From 10:30 to 6:00
   (C) From 10:00 to 6:30
   (D) From 6:00 to 10:30

2. When is the woman usually the busiest at work?
   (A) In the winter
   (B) In the spring
   (C) In the summer
   (D) In the fall

3. Why is the woman surprised?
   (A) The plans for the evening are changed.
   (B) The man made her dinner.
   (C) The man won't share his popcorn.
   (D) She thought it was Thursday, but it's not.

4. Why is the woman annoyed with the man?
   (A) He won't let her go to the meeting.
   (B) He prevented her from completing her work.
   (C) He was late for dinner.
   (D) He burned the popcorn.

5. How late was the man for his appointment?
   (A) Thirty minutes late
   (B) An hour late
   (C) An hour and thirty minutes late
   (D) Two hours late

6. What will happen if the man does not go to his next appointment?
   (A) He will not be allowed to see the doctor.
   (B) He will need to make another appointment.
   (C) He will have to find a new doctor.
   (D) He will have to pay a fee.

DICTATION 2

TRACK 019

A Listen and fill in the blanks.

M What ________ do you begin ________?

W I start ________ at ________ every morning. I like that I don't start ________ ________.

M How ________ do you usually ________?

W ________. On ____________, I sometimes work ________ 8:00 because the ________ stays open ________.

M Do you ever work on ____________?

W Yes, I ________________ put in a half ________.

M What's your ____________ ____________?

W ____________. It's because of the Christmas ____________. While everyone is out ____________, I'm ____________ hard.

B Listen and fill in the blanks.

W Aren't we ________ to the ________________ meeting tonight? It's ____________ ________ to leave. Why are you ____________ popcorn?

M ________, they ________________ the ____________ until next ________.

W Oh, so ________ is the meeting ________?

M It's not until next ____________ at ________.

W How ________ have you known that?

M Brian ____________ me a few hours ago to let me know.

W I really wish you had ________ me ________ of time. It's ________ annoying. I ____________ home from work. I could have ____________ my ____________ instead.

M I'm sorry. I'll ________ it on the ____________ so we don't ____________.

C Listen and fill in the blanks.

M I'd ________ to see Dr. Wilson, ____________.

W Do you ________ an ________________?

M My appointment was at ________.

W It's nearly ________, sir. The ____________ is with his last ____________ of the day.

M I ________, but I got ________ in traffic. Can I see him ________ ________ in the ____________?

W Hmm. Let me ________… Yes, he has an ____________ at 8:30 ____________. But if you miss that ________________ too, we will have to ____________ you a ________.

Unit 3 Feeling Good

KEY WORDS

TRACK 020

Listen for these words.

confused	pleased	disappointed	frustrated	upset
annoyed	worried	surprised	nervous	embarrassed

KEY EXPRESSIONS

TRACK 021

Listen and match each question with its correct answer.

1. What's wrong? •
2. I feel miserable. •
3. Do you ever feel frustrated? •
4. Are you angry at me? •
5. What do you do when you feel lonely? •

• (A) Why? What's the matter?
• (B) I'm not mad. I'm just disappointed.
• (C) I usually call or text one of my friends.
• (D) Yes, especially when I study hard for a test but get a bad grade.
• (E) I'm sick and tired of working six days a week.

Listen and check how the speaker feels.

1. (A) Pleased (B) Worried
2. (A) Disappointed (B) Pleased
3. (A) Upset (B) Excited
4. (A) Embarrassed (B) Surprised
5. (A) Confused (B) Angry

LISTEN FOR IT

Listen and check how the speaker is feeling now.

1. (A) Confused (B) Pleased
2. (A) Frustrated (B) Embarrassed
3. (A) Mad (B) Sad
4. (A) Surprised (B) Disappointed
5. (A) Annoyed (B) Nervous

TRUE OR FALSE

Listen and write T for true or F for false.

1. _______ (A) Exercise helps the man feel less nervous before an exam.
   _______ (B) The man always studies on the morning of an exam.

2. _______ (A) The woman got married today.
   _______ (B) The woman's friend was very happy.

3. _______ (A) The woman was scared during the movie.
   _______ (B) The woman wants to see a funny movie next time.

LISTENING PRACTICE

Listen and choose the correct answer.

1. Why is the woman disappointed?
   (A) The man broke her phone.
   (B) The man forgot about the plans they had made.
   (C) Her mother didn't buy the phone that she wanted.
   (D) Her phone needs to be repaired.

2. What did the man NOT do yesterday afternoon?
   (A) Go somewhere with his mom
   (B) Break something
   (C) Eat ice cream with his mom
   (D) Watch a movie

3. How does the man's job make him feel?
   (A) Frustrated
   (B) Pleased
   (C) Nervous
   (D) Confused

4. What is most difficult about the man's job?
   (A) It involves writing a lot of reports.
   (B) He has to make a lot of presentations.
   (C) It prevents him from spending time with friends.
   (D) He has to work on Sundays most weeks.

5. Who would be interested in this talk?
   (A) People with lots of friends
   (B) People who feel worried about life
   (C) People who are usually happy
   (D) People who like to meet new people

6. What is the man selling?
   (A) A text service
   (B) A new telephone
   (C) A message service
   (D) A book

DICTATION 1 TRACK 026

A Listen and fill in the blanks.

1. We _______ to do a _______ homework assignment, but I didn't _______ the instructions that the _______ gave us.
2. My _______ wants me to stay _______ and _______ a report, but I _______ my _______ that we would go to the _______.
3. My _______ is sick again. She is _______, so I don't _______ she will get _______ this time.
4. My _______ agreed to _______ me a _______. It's _______ news!
5. _______, my sister took my _______ shirt without _______. I'm still _______ at her.

B Listen and fill in the blanks.

M Are you _______ at me? You seem _______.

W I'm not _______. I'm just _______.

M Why? _______ did I do?

W _______ were supposed to come to the _______ _______ yesterday _______. I waited for an _______, but you never _______ up. I tried to _______ and _______ you, but you didn't _______ your phone.

M Oh, no! I'm so _______. Please don't be _______. I _______ all about that. I _______ my _______, and I had to go with my _______ to get it _______. Then she wanted to get _______ _______.

W I _______ that's a good _______. But I _______ wanted to see that _______.

C Listen and fill in the blanks.

W How's your _______ going _______ _______, David?

M It's _______, I guess… _______, it's not _______.

W What's _______?

M I'm _______ _______ _______ of working _______ days a week.

W You _______ that the hours were _______ when you took the _______.

M I know. But I didn't know how _______ it would make me _______. Whenever my _______ or _______ make _______ for the _______, I can't go.

W But you have _______ off.

M I know, but my friends _______ want to do _______ on _______.

LISTENING TEST

TRACK 027

Listen and choose the correct answer.

1. How does the woman feel?
   (A) Bored and miserable
   (B) Frustrated and miserable
   (C) Tired and frustrated
   (D) Pleased and surprised

2. What does the man think the woman should do?
   (A) Study harder next time
   (B) Quit her biology class
   (C) Ask her teacher for study tips
   (D) Get a new teacher

3. Why is Miss Parker disappointed in Bill?
   (A) He cheated on a test.
   (B) He failed a test.
   (C) He took her test paper.
   (D) He told her a lie about Sam.

4. What can be inferred about Bill?
   (A) He is not a smart student.
   (B) He could do well if he worked hard.
   (C) He is the best student in the class.
   (D) He is not friends with Sam.

5. When does Karen feel nervous?
   (A) While meeting new people
   (B) While taking exams
   (C) When in crowds
   (D) During public speaking

6. What does Karen tell the man to do?
   (A) Change to a different class
   (B) Come to listen to her presentation
   (C) Try to talk to more people
   (D) Practice his presentation in front of a mirror

DICTATION 2

A Listen and fill in the blanks.

W I feel ________________.

M Why? What's _______?

W Well, do you _______ feel ________________?

M Yes, especially when I _______ hard for a _______ but get a _______ _______.

W ___________. I worked really _______ for my biology _______, but when I looked at the ________________, I couldn't ___________ anything.

M You ___________ did better than you _______.

W No, I ___________ got my result. I ___________.

M Then you need to _______ to your ___________. Maybe she can give you some ___________ on how to _______ _______ ________________.

W I guess. I'm just ________________ to talk to her when I got such a _______ _______.

M No, I'm sure she'll be _______ to help you.

B Listen and fill in the blanks.

W Bill, you got _______% on this _______.

M Did I really? I'm really ________________!

W Yes, I am very ________________ as well. I have to ask you ________________, Bill. Did you copy your ___________ from Sam's _______? You were ___________ next to him, and your ___________ are almost the _______ as his.

M Um, well, yes. I'm ___________ I did, Miss Parker. I didn't have _______ to _______ for the test.

W Oh Bill! You're smart ___________ to _______ this test without ___________.

M I'm sorry, Miss Parker. I've never cheated ___________, and I feel very _______.

C Listen and fill in the blanks.

M _______ do you get ___________, Karen?

W Nervous? I suppose when I have to _______ in front of a _______ of ___________.

M Me, too. I have to give a ________________ in class _______ _______, and I really don't want to.

W I'm _______ I don't have to do that. But my ___________ gave me some good ___________ last year. _______ said I should ___________ my ________________ in front of a ___________.

M _______ to myself _______ _______ _______ a mirror? That sounds _______!

W No, it really helps. Practice ___________, and time how _______ it takes. It will make you feel less ___________, and it will _______ you make sure your ________________ is the right length.

M Hmm, _______ I'll try that.

I Love It!

KEY WORDS

Listen for these words and phrases.

can't stand	love	used to	feel like	hate
healthy	prefer	rude	interested in	wait in line

KEY EXPRESSIONS

Listen and match each question with its correct answer.

1. Do you like reading?
2. How did you like that book I lent you?
3. What is something that annoys you?
4. What do you like to do on the weekend?
5. Do you have any hobbies?

(A) I can't stand rude people.
(B) It was awful.
(C) Oh, yes. I love to read.
(D) I'm into photography these days.
(E) It depends. I tend to stay at home, but sometimes I go out to a nice restaurant.

WARM-UP

TRACK 031

Listen and check what the speaker dislikes.

1. (A) People who make appointments (B) People who are late for appointments
2. (A) Her brother (B) Rock music
3. (A) Going out (B) Saturdays
4. (A) Pizza (B) Healthy food
5. (A) Cooking (B) Eating out

LISTEN FOR IT

Listen and check what the speaker likes.

1. (A) Walking in the rain (B) Staying at home on a rainy day
2. (A) Studying math (B) Reading
3. (A) Being a nurse (B) Helping people
4. (A) Swimming in a pool (B) Swimming in the sea
5. (A) Getting up early (B) Getting up late

TRUE OR FALSE

Listen and write T for true or F for false.

1. ______ (A) The man likes all kinds of music.
   ______ (B) The man listens to music all day.

2. ______ (A) The woman and her husband both like to watch dramas.
   ______ (B) The woman's husband hates cooking shows.

3. ______ (A) The man is interested in learning a new language.
   ______ (B) The man has never been to China.

LISTENING PRACTICE

Listen and choose the correct answer.

1. What does the woman like to read?
   (A) Detective stories
   (B) Fiction
   (C) Magazines
   (D) Novels

2. What does the man enjoy reading?
   (A) Nature magazines
   (B) Fiction
   (C) Nonfiction
   (D) Fashion magazines

3. What makes the woman angry at traffic lights?
   (A) Lights that take a long time to change
   (B) Red lights
   (C) Broken traffic lights
   (D) Drivers who don't notice the green lights

4. Which is NOT something that annoys the woman?
   (A) People who wait in line
   (B) People who are rude
   (C) People who use a phone in their car
   (D) People who use a phone in a movie theater

5. How does the woman feel about going to restaurants?
   (A) It's too expensive.
   (B) It's boring.
   (C) It's difficult in a small town.
   (D) It's a great way to try healthy foods.

6. Why does the man like going to restaurants?
   (A) He hates to cook.
   (B) He doesn't have a kitchen.
   (C) He likes trying new kinds of food.
   (D) He doesn't like healthy foods.

A Listen and fill in the blanks.

1. The ________ way to ________ a ________ day is to sit on the ________ and read a ________ ________.
2. A lot of my ____________ hate ________, but I love to ________ math. It's more ________________ than reading.
3. It makes me very ________ when I ________ other ____________. Because of this, I'm thinking about ____________ a ________.
4. My favorite ________ to go is the ________. I can ________ in the sea, which is much ____________ ________ a ________.
5. I always ________ ________ early because it makes me feel ________ ________ ____________. I love ____________ the sun rise.

B Listen and fill in the blanks.

M ________, do you like ____________?

W Oh yes, I ________ to read.

M Do you ________ a lot of ____________?

W Not really. I only read ________________ because I prefer to ________ something ________ while I am ____________. And to be ____________, I read more ________________ than ________.

M ________ magazines do you like?

W I'm ________ ________ fashion magazines and nature magazines. I ________ to read about ________________ ____________. How ________ you? Do you ________ a lot?

M I ________ ________ magazines, but I do like to read ________________ ____________.

C Listen and fill in the blanks.

What is ________________ that ____________ you? I can't stand ________ ____________. For example, I ________ people who ________ to ________ in front when I am ____________ ________ ________. Please ________! I also hate people who use their ________ when they are ____________ at a ____________ ________. The light goes ________ and their car doesn't ________. They are ________ ________ looking at their ________, and they don't see the light ____________. It's rude behavior! ________ looking at your phone, ____________! Oh, and don't use your phone ________ you are at the movie ____________. It's annoying to see the ________ from your ________ when I ________ ________ to watch the ________.

LISTENING TEST

TRACK 036

Listen and choose the correct answer.

1. What are the man and woman mainly discussing?
   (A) A movie they both saw
   (B) A book they both read
   (C) An actress they both like
   (D) A place they both visited

2. What did the woman dislike about Ruby?
   (A) Her hair was too long.
   (B) She was not a nice person.
   (C) She was rude to the woman.
   (D) She didn't say anything interesting.

3. What does the woman think about the man's hobby?
   (A) It's probably expensive.
   (B) It's probably interesting.
   (C) It's probably difficult.
   (D) It's probably not popular.

4. What does the man do with his photos?
   (A) Print them for his friends
   (B) Delete them all
   (C) Use an online album
   (D) Sell them on the internet

5. What are the man and woman discussing?
   (A) What time to leave
   (B) What to eat for dinner
   (C) Where to watch a movie
   (D) How to spend the evening

6. What does the woman NOT say about movies?
   (A) She downloaded two movies.
   (B) She wants to watch movies at home.
   (C) She only wants to watch a serious movie.
   (D) The movies she downloaded will make the man laugh.

DICTATION 2

TRACK 037

A Listen and fill in the blanks.

M _______ did you like that _______ I _______ you?

W It was _______. I don't know _______ you _______ it to me.

M You _______ so? I thought it was _______________. What didn't you _______ about it?

W Well, for one thing, it was so _______. I ___________ reading _______ stories. And I didn't like the _______ character, _______. She was very _______ and unfriendly. I wasn't _______________ _______ finding out what ___________ to her.

M I'm _______ that you didn't like it. I was going to _______________ another book, but _______ that's not a good idea.

W I ___________ like the _______ you suggest, so go _______.

B Listen and fill in the blanks.

W Do you _______ any ___________?

M I'm into _______________ these _______.

W That ___________ like an _______________ hobby.

M Not ___________. I mean, the ___________ was a little _______________, but I didn't buy a _______ one. You don't _______ to buy the _______ ___________ to take good photos.

W Do you _______ out your ___________?

M No, I _______ at them on my ___________, or I _______ them with my ___________ online. I think it's a _______ of _______ to _______ out lots of ___________.

W Yeah. And that would be _______________ as well.

C Listen and fill in the blanks.

M Would _______ like to do _______________ tonight?

W I don't feel like _______ _______. Can we just hang out at _______?

M _______. Let's _______ a movie.

W A _______ sounds good. I _______________ a couple of ___________ the other day. Why don't we _______ one of _______?

M As long as they're _______ _______ serious. I'd like to _______ something _______.

W Not a ___________. They are both ___________. I heard that they are both ___________ _______, so I think you'll _______ _______ both.

M Great. Let's _______ them _______.

Working Life

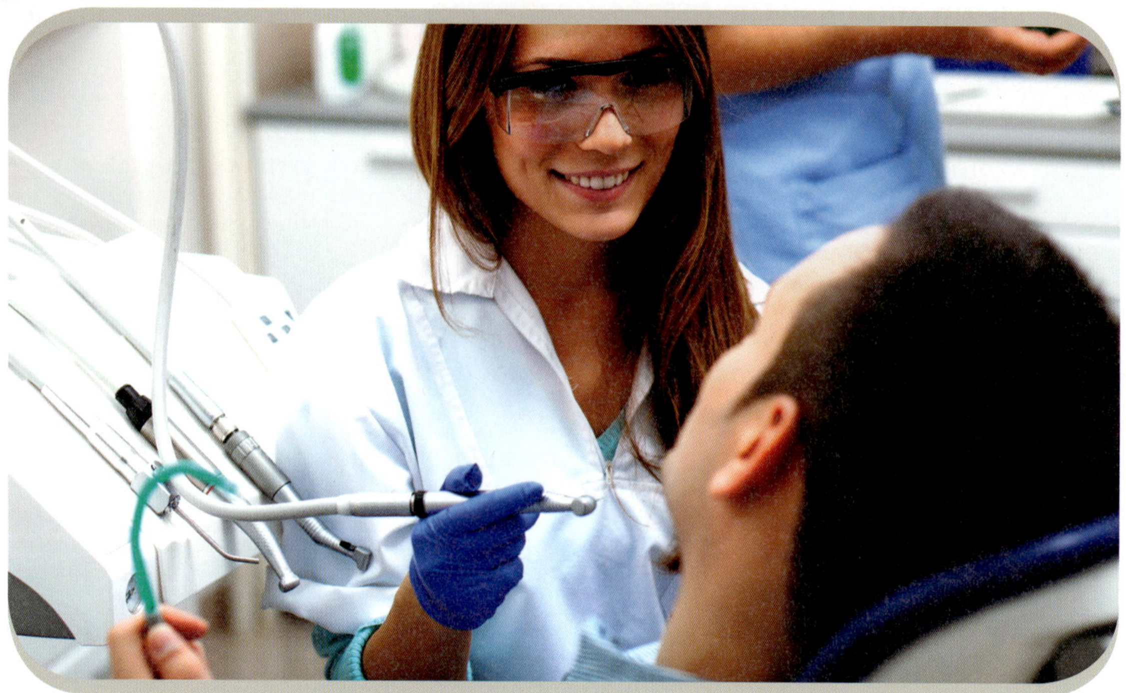

KEY WORDS

TRACK 038

Listen for these words and phrases.

business person	doctor	architect	plumber	pension
dentist	employer	promotion	benefit	gardener

KEY EXPRESSIONS

Listen and match each question with its correct answer.

1. Is your job stressful?
2. How long have you been a teacher?
3. What do you do exactly?
4. Who do you work for?
5. How much vacation time do you get?

(A) I work for ABC Technology.
(B) I get ten paid days off a year.
(C) I've been teaching since 2015.
(D) Only when I have a big project to complete.
(E) I sell new products to stores.

WARM-UP

TRACK 040

Listen and check how the speaker feels about his or her job.

1. (A) Satisfied (B) Bored
2. (A) Excited (B) Frustrated
3. (A) Disappointed (B) Excited
4. (A) Nervous (B) Angry
5. (A) Tired (B) Surprised

LISTEN FOR IT

Listen and check what kind of job would be good for the speaker.

1. (A) Shoe store clerk (B) Book store clerk
2. (A) Gardener (B) Plumber
3. (A) Teacher (B) Doctor
4. (A) Plumber (B) Business person
5. (A) Dentist (B) Architect

TRUE OR FALSE

Listen and write T for true or F for false.

1. _______ (A) The woman goes to work by bus.
   _______ (B) Customers often say she is too slow.

2. _______ (A) The man thinks his salary is good.
   _______ (B) The man wishes he had more time off.

3. _______ (A) The woman has done many different kinds of jobs.
   _______ (B) The woman's father used to be a writer.

LISTENING PRACTICE

Listen and choose the correct answer.

1. How long has the woman had her job?
   (A) Three years
   (B) Four years
   (C) Five years
   (D) Six years

2. What does the woman like about her job?
   (A) Staying in her office all day
   (B) Meeting lots of people
   (C) Learning new skills
   (D) Designing new products

3. What happened to the woman's father?
   (A) He lost his job.
   (B) He moved to a different company.
   (C) He got a promotion.
   (D) He started a new company.

4. Which of the following is a negative aspect of her father's position?
   (A) He gets paid more.
   (B) He has many supervisors.
   (C) The company gave him a car.
   (D) He works longer hours.

5. When did the man first decide to become a teacher?
   (A) In 2015
   (B) When he was a child
   (C) A few years ago
   (D) In second grade

6. What does the man like about his job?
   (A) Being able to have long vacations
   (B) Being able to work indoors
   (C) Being able to meet other teachers
   (D) Being able to teach skills to young children

A Listen and fill in the blanks.

1. I love __________, so it would be ______ to be around ______ all ______.
2. I've __________ been good at __________ __________ and plants. I also enjoy being __________.
3. My ______ subjects in __________ are math and __________, especially biology. I also like __________ people, so I want to ______ in a __________.
4. I ______ ______ to work in an __________ or ______ things. I ______ I'd be good at __________ things.
5. My ______ is to design __________ ______________. Most schools are ______, so I want to make ______________ schools where everyone wants to ______.

B Listen and fill in the blanks.

M ______ do you ______ for?

W I ______ for ABC Technology. I've been ______ for about ______ ______.

M ______ do you do __________?

W I ______ new products to ________ in three different ______. We __________ computer accessories, so it's my ______ to persuade __________ to ______ our products.

M Do you ______ it?

W Yes, I get to ______ a lot of __________, and I have to ______ a lot of ________ every day, so I don't ______ the day __________ at a ______. It's fun to __________ our ______ __________ to other people.

M That __________ like an ______________ ______.

C Listen and fill in the blanks.

My __________ recently got a ______________ at ______. He works __________ ______, so we are all ______ of him. He ______ from assistant __________ to executive manager at the ______________ __________ where he works. He got a ______ increase of ______%, and he is now ______ __________ of more __________. He also gets a __________ ______ now. He used to ______________ ______ people, but ______ he is in charge of ______ people. He has a lot more ______ to do. He seems to work __________ ______ now, and I think he has a bit more __________, but I'm sure he will ______ ______ to it.

Listen and choose the correct answer.

1. Where is this conversation taking place?
   (A) In a doctor's office
   (B) In a vacation resort
   (C) At a party
   (D) At a train station

2. What does the woman think that the man should do?
   (A) Exercise more
   (B) Find a new job
   (C) Become a plumber
   (D) Work fewer hours

3. How much vacation time will the woman get this year?
   (A) Ten days
   (B) Twelve days
   (C) Fifteen days
   (D) Six months

4. Which of the following is NOT a benefit of the woman's job?
   (A) Free food
   (B) Pension
   (C) Reduced prices at a gym
   (D) Company car

5. What can be inferred about the speakers?
   (A) They work together.
   (B) They are meeting for the first time.
   (C) They are old school friends.
   (D) They live next to each other.

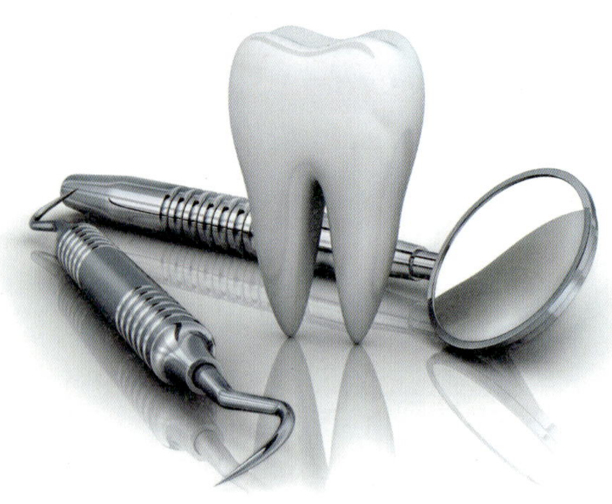

6. What does Liz do for a living?
   (A) Gardener
   (B) Dentist
   (C) Dental assistant
   (D) Classroom assistant

DICTATION 2

TRACK 046

A Listen and fill in the blanks.

W OK, Mr. Smith. Well, you ________ ________ ________ generally healthy, but your ________ is a little ________. Is your job ______________?

M ________ when I have a big ____________ to complete. I'm a ____________ and most of my ________ are ________. But I ________ ________ myself, not an ____________, so it's sometimes ________________ to take a break or a ____________.

W How many ________ do you ________ without a ________?

M Most ________ I work from ________ a.m. until ________ p.m., but if the job is ________________, I might have to work ________ as late as ________ at ________.

W I see. Well, I ________ you need to ________ taking some more ____________, for your ____________.

B Listen and fill in the blanks.

M ________ ________ have you ________ with your ____________, Daniella?

W For about ________ ____________.

M How do you ________ it ________ ________?

W It's going ________. I'm really ________ that I studied ____________ studies. It is really ____________ me to be a good ____________ ____________.

M How much ____________ time do you get?

W I get ________ paid days off a year, but that will ____________ to ____________ after ________ years, and ____________ days after three.

M Do you get any ____________?

W There is a company ____________, and I can get a ____________ on a gym membership. And there is ________ ________________ in the staff ________ ________.

C Listen and fill in the blanks.

M ________ time no see, Liz.

W Felix! It's great to see you. I ________ that you ____________ a ________________ ____________.

M That's ________. I love ________________, so I thought I ________ as well ________ ________ to do it. So now I ________ my own ____________. There are ________ of us working as ________________.

W Nice. I ________ ________ Johnson Dental ____________—the one on ________ Street.

M Oh ____________? Are you a dental ________________?

W Actually, I'm a ____________.

M Oh, ________ ________! That's great. You ____________ were the ________ one in the ________!

School Life

KEY WORDS

Listen for these words and phrases.

medical school	law	literature	cram (for an exam)	university
bachelor's degree	social studies	chemistry	graduate school	tuition fees

KEY EXPRESSIONS

Listen and match each question with its correct answer.

1. What year are you in?
2. How many classes are you taking this semester?
3. What grade did you get on the last test?
4. What do you want to do after you graduate?
5. Did you get into medical school?

(A) I got a B.
(B) Yes, I start in the fall.
(C) I think I'll probably go to graduate school.
(D) I'm taking three classes this time.
(E) I'm a senior.

WARM-UP

Listen and check what the speaker plans to study.

1. (A) Writing (B) Literature
2. (A) Medicine (B) Nursing
3. (A) Chemistry (B) Medicine
4. (A) Culture (B) Social studies
5. (A) Law (B) Chemistry

LISTEN FOR IT

Listen and check the subject the speaker liked best in school.

1. (A) P.E. (B) Social studies
2. (A) Math (B) English
3. (A) Law (B) Chemistry
4. (A) History (B) Math
5. (A) English (B) Art

TRUE OR FALSE

Listen and write T for true or F for false.

1. _______ (A) The man was disappointed with his grades.
   _______ (B) The man often gets bad grades.

2. _______ (A) The woman's brother will soon finish university.
   _______ (B) Robin thinks graduate school is too expensive.

3. _______ (A) The man is a high school student.
   _______ (B) The man studies in the library.

LISTENING PRACTICE

Listen and choose the correct answer.

1. What is the main topic of the dialog?
   (A) What the woman studied in college
   (B) What the man will study in college
   (C) Where the man will attend college
   (D) How long the man will attend college

2. Which of the following is NOT a subject mentioned by the man?
   (A) Chemistry
   (B) Math
   (C) English
   (D) Biology

3. Why didn't the man study for his exam?
   (A) He forgot that he had an exam.
   (B) He thinks the class is boring.
   (C) He is very good at social studies.
   (D) His teacher said he didn't need to study.

4. How will the man feel if he gets a C on the exam?
   (A) Disappointed
   (B) Surprised
   (C) Bored
   (D) Satisfied

5. Which of the following is NOT true about the woman?
   (A) She is going to change her major next semester.
   (B) She lives near the university.
   (C) She is having fun at university.
   (D) She is still deciding what to do after graduation.

6. What can be inferred about the woman?
   (A) She is a senior.
   (B) She is not a great student.
   (C) She is a freshman.
   (D) She is not good at math.

DICTATION 1

A Listen and fill in the blanks.

1. I wasn't _______ at _______ or ___________, but I really enjoyed ___________ _______ when I was a ___________.
2. The only _______ I was _______ at in ___________ was math, but ___________ was my favorite.
3. I liked _______________ the most in _______ ___________ because I liked doing _______________.
4. I was _______ a very good ___________, but I did enjoy ___________. I had a _______ ___________.
5. I used to _______ classes where I could _______ _______________. That's _______ I enjoyed _______ so much.

B Listen and fill in the blanks.

W _______ year are you in?

M I'm a ___________.

W In ___________?

M _______, I'm still in _______ ___________, but I'm going to college _______ _______.

W Do you _______ what you will _______ in ___________?

M I _______ to go to ___________ ___________ eventually, so I ___________ to get a _______________ ___________ in chemistry first. I'll _______ take a lot of _______ and ___________ classes, of course.

W It ___________ like you have ___________ out your ___________ well.

M I hope so, but I _______ that I have a lot of _______ to do if I want to ___________.

W Well, _______ _______, Simon.

C Listen and fill in the blanks.

I have a _______ exam ___________. It's for my ___________ ___________ class. I find the _______ a bit ___________, so I didn't really _______ much. Now I have to _______ _______ the exam ___________. My ___________ all say that it's _______ to _______ for an _______. I think they are probably _______ because I forget _______________ that I learned right after the _______. Maybe I would ___________ more if I ___________ more _______________ over several _______. Anyway, it's _______ _______ now! Wish me luck, because I'm going to _______ it! It's OK if I get a _______. I just don't want to _______.

LISTENING TEST

TRACK 054

Listen and choose the correct answer.

1. How many classes is the woman taking this semester?

   (A) One (B) Two
   (C) Three (D) Four

2. What subject will the man and woman study together?

   (A) History (B) Korean
   (C) French (D) Chemistry

3. What is the woman worried about?

   (A) Getting into medical school
   (B) Graduating from medical school
   (C) Paying for medical school
   (D) Finding a place to live near medical school

4. Why does the man think that the woman does not need to worry?

   (A) She will earn a good salary after medical school.
   (B) She will get good grades in medical school.
   (C) It's easy to get into medical school.
   (D) Her parents have lots of money.

5. What can be inferred about the man and the woman?

   (A) They are in the same class.
   (B) They both find math very difficult.
   (C) They are meeting for the first time.
   (D) They are both teachers at the same school.

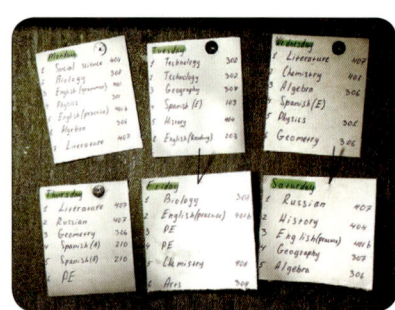

6. How did the man feel about his last grade?

   (A) Pleased (B) Excited
   (C) Disappointed (D) Bored

DICTATION 2

A Listen and fill in the blanks.

W ______ many ________ are you ________?
M I'm taking ______ this time. I was going to take ________ but decided ________ it.
W ______ you taking __________? I was ________ we could be ______ ________.
M Yes, I'm taking __________, ________, and a ______ class.
W OK, I'm ________ chemistry and ________. Have you taken ________?
M No, but I took ________ last year. It was really ______ to learn a ______ ______ of ________.
W That sounds ________ __________. French is hard ________ for me, and that uses the same ________ as ________!

B Listen and fill in the blanks.

M Hey, Miranda! Did you get into ________ ________?
W Yes, I ______ in the ______.
M Wow, that's ______. You must be so ________.
W Yeah, but now I'm ________ about the ________ ______.
M But you ______ it was __________ when you ________.
W ______, I did, but I didn't really ______ that I would be ________. So now I have to ________ a lot of ______ to ______ for my ________.
M But that's ________ for medical ________. All your __________ will have to do the ______. It's ______. You'll make lots of ______ after you ________.

C Listen and fill in the blanks.

M Have you ________ the ______ ________, Sonya?
W ______ quite, but I'm ________ ______.
M Can you ______ me with a ________ of the ________? I don't __________ how to do them.
W Sure. Hey, what ______ did you get on the ______ ______?
M I got a ______, but I really ________ an ______.
W I can ______ you ______ for the next ______ if you like. I'm doing really ______ in this ______.
M That would be ______.
W Let's get ________ to ______, then go to the ________ for a ______?
M Sure. It's ______ to ______ when I'm ________!

A New Home

KEY WORDS

Listen for these words and phrases.

realtor	townhouse	upstairs	studio apartment	view
redecorate	air conditioner	recently	furniture	condominium

KEY EXPRESSIONS

Listen and match each question with its correct answer.

1. Do you mind if I turn down the air conditioner?
2. Do you live in the city?
3. How long have you lived here?
4. Have you finished redecorating your new place?
5. Have you met your neighbors?

(A) Yes, we went and introduced ourselves when we first moved in.
(B) Almost, but there are still a few things to do.
(C) No, I recently moved to the suburbs.
(D) Of course not. Go ahead.
(E) We've been in this house for about three years.

WARM-UP TRACK 058

Listen and check where the speaker lives.

1. (A) Apartment (B) Townhouse
2. (A) Country (B) Suburbs
3. (A) Apartment (B) Condominium
4. (A) Townhouse (B) Studio apartment
5. (A) City (B) Suburbs

LISTEN FOR IT TRACK 059

Listen and check which room the speaker is talking about.

1. (A) Bathroom (B) Kitchen
2. (A) Living room (B) Hallway
3. (A) Dining room (B) Bedroom
4. (A) Play room (B) Living room
5. (A) Bedroom (B) Bathroom

TRUE OR FALSE TRACK 060

Listen and write T for true or F for false.

1. ______ (A) The man is painting the walls of his new home.
   ______ (B) The man lives in the city.

2. ______ (A) A realtor is showing a house to a client.
   ______ (B) The kitchen needs new cupboards.

3. ______ (A) The man is hoping to sell his house soon.
   ______ (B) The man's house has three bedrooms.

LISTENING PRACTICE

Listen and choose the correct answer.

1. What new things did the man buy for his bedroom?
   (A) A bed and table
   (B) A table and drawers
   (C) A bed and drawers
   (D) A bed and chair

2. What does the woman think the man should do?
   (A) Paint the walls green
   (B) Paint the walls blue
   (C) Paint the walls purple
   (D) Paint the walls blue and green

3. Why does the man like living in a townhouse?
   (A) It has a lot of stairs.
   (B) It has a great view.
   (C) It is cheap.
   (D) He has no neighbors next door.

4. What does the woman think the man should do?
   (A) Invite his neighbors to his house
   (B) Move to a house with fewer stairs
   (C) Move to a better neighborhood
   (D) Introduce himself to his neighbors

5. What can be inferred about the man?
   (A) He went to high school with the man.
   (B) He lives next door to the woman.
   (C) He has not visited the woman's house before.
   (D) He is a realtor.

6. Who is Sheila Kim?
   (A) Someone the man works with
   (B) Someone who can help the man find a house to buy
   (C) Someone who lives in the man's condominium
   (D) Someone who wants to meet the man

DICTATION 1 TRACK 062

A Listen and fill in the blanks.

1. Do you like the ________ ________ and ________? It's so much more fun to ________ now!
2. I bought new ________ to ________ my new ________. My new ________ and ________ are very ________.
3. Thanks to my new ________, I finally ________ well at ________.
4. My ________ are ________ because they have a ________ where they can ________ and ________ with all their ________.
5. The ________ and ________ are both new. The ________ gives the room lots of ________.

B Listen and fill in the blanks.

W Have you ________ ________ your ________?

M Almost, but there are still a few ________ to do. The ________ already ________ the ________ and ________. But we still need to ________ the ________.

W What ________ are you ________ them?

M Actually, it's ________ to ________. I think ________ would be ________, but my ________ wants to ________ them ________.

W Why don't you paint ________ ________ one color, and paint the ________ wall the ________ ________? It's ________ these days.

M That's an ________ ________.

W Plus, ________ and ________ look good ________. It'll ________ ________.

C Listen and fill in the blanks.

W So this is a ________?

M Yes, I ________ it because I have a ________ ________ from the ________ ________.

W But you have to go ________ and ________ again ________ ________ a day.

M It's ________ for me.

W There are too ________ ________ for me. It seems very ________. Have you ________ your ________?

M Yes, we went and ________ ________ when we first ________ ________. They seem ________.

W You should ________ them to ________.

M We ________ will.

LISTENING TEST

Listen and choose the correct answer.

1. Why did the man move to the suburbs?
   - (A) He doesn't want to live near the woman.
   - (B) It's better for his dog.
   - (C) It's cheaper than the city.
   - (D) It's closer to where he works.

2. Which of the following is NOT near the man's house?
   - (A) A theater
   - (B) A library
   - (C) A park
   - (D) Tennis courts

3. What does the woman like about her job?
   - (A) Decorating other people's houses
   - (B) Helping people
   - (C) Earning a lot of money
   - (D) Visiting other people's houses

4. What does the woman dislike about her job?
   - (A) Meeting a lot of people
   - (B) Visiting houses that are too hot
   - (C) Looking at ugly houses
   - (D) Buying houses

5. Where is this conversation taking place?
   - (A) In an office
   - (B) At a restaurant
   - (C) At the man's house
   - (D) At the woman's house

6. How many rooms does the man have?
   - (A) Two
   - (B) Three
   - (C) Four
   - (D) Five

A Listen and fill in the blanks.

W Do you _______ in the _______, Tom?

M No, I _______ _______ to the _______.

W I _______ think about _______ to the suburbs. I have a _______ _______ in the _______ _______.

M I used to _______ an _______ _______, but I wanted more _______. I have a _______, so an apartment wasn't _______ for him.

W So where do you _______?

M I have a _______ on Freeport Road, _______ the _______.

W That's a _______ _______. I sometimes go for _______ in that _______.

M Yes, it's very _______, and there is a _______ _______ with _______ courts near my _______.

B Listen and fill in the blanks.

M What do you do _______ _______ _______, Soo Kyung?

W I'm a _______. I help _______ _______ and _______ _______.

M What do you like _______ about your _______?

W I like _______ _______ other people's houses. It's very _______. It gives me _______ _______ _______ for _______ my _______ _______.

M But I'm _______ you _______ some _______ houses, too.

W I do, and I _______ _______ houses that don't have _______ _______ in the _______. But _______ of the time, I really _______ my job.

M It _______ _______.

C Listen and fill in the blanks.

M _______ in. _______ almost _______.

W I'm _______ I'm _______. I had some _______ _______ your house.

M Yes, the _______ can be a little _______ around here.

W How many _______ do you have?

M _______. The _______ is _______ that _______, and my bedroom's over there.

W Where's the _______?

M In _______. Why don't you have a _______?

W OK. Your _______ looks _______.

Places to Go

KEY WORDS

TRACK 065

Listen for these words and phrases.

reservation	passport	cruise	confirm	aisle seat
boarding pass	carry-on	travel agent	hotel lobby	beach resort

KEY EXPRESSIONS

Listen and match each question with its correct answer.

1. I'd like to confirm a flight, please.
2. Have you ever been abroad?
3. Would you like a window or an aisle seat?
4. May I see your passport, please?
5. What time should I check out?

(A) Here you are.
(B) Certainly. Can I have your name and flight number?
(C) Check out is at 11:00 a.m.
(D) Aisle, please.
(E) Yes, I went to Europe last year.

WARM-UP

Listen and check where the speaker is going on vacation.

1. (A) Beach resort (B) City hotel
2. (A) France (B) Summer school
3. (A) Disneyland (B) Mountains
4. (A) Cruise (B) Beach resort
5. (A) India (B) Italy

LISTEN FOR IT

Listen and check where the speaker went for their last vacation.

1. (A) Europe (B) Asia
2. (A) Thailand (B) Cambodia
3. (A) A hotel (B) Nowhere
4. (A) The United States (B) Europe
5. (A) China (B) Antartica

TRUE OR FALSE

Listen and write T for true or F for false.

1. _______ (A) The man is probably a travel agent.
   _______ (B) The man has tickets for a trip in the United States.

2. _______ (A) The woman did not have a good time in Hong Kong.
   _______ (B) The woman spent a lot of money during her vacation.

3. _______ (A) It is a lot more expensive for the woman to take an airplane.
   _______ (B) The woman will need to transfer in Dallas.

LISTENING PRACTICE

Listen and choose the correct answer.

1. Where is this conversation taking place?
   (A) At a travel agent's office
   (B) On an airplane
   (C) At an airport
   (D) On the telephone

2. How does the man feel about the change to his travel plans?
   (A) Annoyed
   (B) Pleased
   (C) Frustrated
   (D) Sad

3. Which city did the woman NOT visit last year?
   (A) London
   (B) Paris
   (C) Rome
   (D) Milan

4. What kind of transportation did the woman use in Europe?
   (A) Bus
   (B) Ferry
   (C) Train
   (D) Bicycle

5. Where is this conversation taking place?
   (A) On a cruise ship
   (B) At an airport
   (C) In a travel agency
   (D) At a bus station

6. What time will the man's flight leave?
   (A) In 20 minutes
   (B) At 11:15
   (C) At 11:22
   (D) At 12:00

DICTATION 1

TRACK 071

A Listen and fill in the blanks.

1. I spent _____ weeks on a _____ ship last _____. I stopped in _____, Portugal, Italy, and _____.
2. I _____ got a _____ in Thailand, so I spent my last _____ in _____ because it is near there.
3. I don't like _____ because I don't like _____, so I _____ at _____ last year.
4. My _____ in _____ _____ and Boston was so much _____ last winter, even though it was _____.
5. I went to _____ my _____ who lives in _____ a couple of _____ ago. It was great.

B Listen and fill in the blanks.

W _____. Giselle's Travel.

M I'd _____ to _____ a _____, please.

W Can I have your _____ and _____ _____?

M Yes, it's Jonathon Fielding, _____ _____.

W OK, you're _____, Mr. Fielding, on Flight 755 for this _____ _____. Please note that the _____ time has _____.

M Oh, really?

W Yes, the _____ now _____ London Heathrow at _____ instead of 8:00. You will _____ in Seoul _____ minutes _____ than originally scheduled.

M That's even _____! I can _____ a little longer on _____.

C Listen and fill in the blanks.

M _____ you _____ been _____?

W Yes. I went to _____ last _____.

M How was it? What _____ did you _____?

W I _____ to Paris, then I took a _____ to Milan and _____. It was _____.

M Didn't you visit _____? I've always _____ to go _____.

W _____, I didn't have _____ time, but I did go _____ Switzerland on the _____. The _____ of the _____ was _____.

M I'd really like to _____ another _____ someday. I _____ to save up _____ money first.

Listen and choose the correct answer.

1. How does the woman feel when she sees the resort?
   (A) Tired
   (B) Disappointed
   (C) Confused
   (D) Frustrated

2. What does the woman want to find out?
   (A) Whether or not the hotel serves breakfast
   (B) Whether or not she needs to pay for breakfast
   (C) What time the hotel serves breakfast
   (D) What food the hotel offers for breakfast

3. Where is this conversation taking place?
   (A) At an airport
   (B) On a cruise ship
   (C) At a bus station
   (D) At Hotel Windsor

4. Who is the woman traveling with?
   (A) Her husband
   (B) Her mother
   (C) Her children
   (D) Her best friend

5. What kind of room did the woman reserve?
   (A) A smoking room
   (B) A room on the first floor
   (C) A room for two people
   (D) A room with a view of the ocean

6. Which of the following times is NOT acceptable for the woman to check out?
   (A) 10:00 a.m.
   (B) 10:45 a.m.
   (C) 11:00 a.m.
   (D) 11:20 a.m.

A Listen and fill in the blanks.

M Oh, ________, Ji-Min! There's a ________ for the beach ____________. And here is the resort.

W It's ________ than I ____________. It looked much ____________ in the pictures that ________ ____________ showed us.

M It looks ________ to me. Why don't you ________ here in the ________ ________ while I check in?

W No, I'll ________ with you. They'll probably need to see my ____________, and I have a few ________________.

M I ________ you aren't going to ____________ about ____________.

W No, of ____________ not. I want to ask about ________________. I can't ____________ if it is ____________ in the price or not.

M I ________ it's included, but you can ________.

B Listen and fill in the blanks.

M Good ____________, ma'am. May I see your ____________ ________ and ____________?

W ________ you are. I have my ________________ passports as well. For my ________ and my daughter.

M Thank you. ________ are you ________________ from?

W We ________ in from ____________. We're going on a ____________.

M I see. ________ ________ will you be here in ____________?

W Just one ________. Our cruise leaves ____________.

M And can you ________ me the ____________ of the ________ where you are ____________ tonight?

W Yes. It's ________ Windsor, Chancery Lane.

C Listen and fill in the blanks.

W Hello, I have a ________________ under the ________ Samantha Baker.

M Ah, yes, Miss Baker. You are ____________ with us for ________ ____________.

W That's ________.

M I see you ____________ a non-smoking ________ with an ________ view. A single ________. That all looks ________. You are in room ________, which is on the 7th ________.

W Great. What ________ should I ________ ________?

M Check out is at ________ a.m.

Plans and Appointments

KEY WORDS

TRACK 074

Listen for these words and phrases.

appointment	cancel	available	free	urgent
suit	run late	arrange	picnic	date

KEY EXPRESSIONS

Listen and match each question with its correct answer.

1. Are you free this evening?	(A) I'll try to go.
2. Are you coming to the picnic tomorrow?	(B) Come to my apartment any time after 6:00.
3. What time should I come?	(C) That sounds like fun.
4. Have you arranged food for the party?	(D) No, I have to study for a math exam tonight.
5. How about going to a baseball game next week?	(E) Yes, my mom and her friends are going to cook.

WARM-UP

Listen and check what the speaker has to do today.

1. (A) Arrange a party (B) Buy a gift
2. (A) Make an appointment (B) Cancel an appointment
3. (A) Take an English exam (B) Give a presentation
4. (A) Cook something (B) Buy a cake
5. (A) Nothing special (B) Go on vacation

LISTEN FOR IT

Listen and check why the speaker had to cancel their plans.

1. (A) He is sick. (B) His mom won't let him go.
2. (A) The weather is bad. (B) Her friend hurt his leg.
3. (A) He is too busy. (B) He is sick.
4. (A) She has to work. (B) She lost her report.
5. (A) He doesn't have any money. (B) He is too tired.

TRUE OR FALSE

Listen and write T for true or F for false.

1. _______ (A) The man is still at work.
   _______ (B) He will meet Sherry at a restaurant.
2. _______ (A) The man wants to go out tonight.
   _______ (B) The man promised to meet Barbara for dinner.
3. _______ (A) The man is probably Mr. Livingston's secretary.
   _______ (B) Mr. Livingston has several appointments tomorrow.

LISTENING PRACTICE

Listen and choose the correct answer.

1. Why is Susan calling Mike?
   (A) To invite him to a movie
   (B) To tell him about a concert
   (C) To ask him about Blake
   (D) To introduce him to Allie Felix

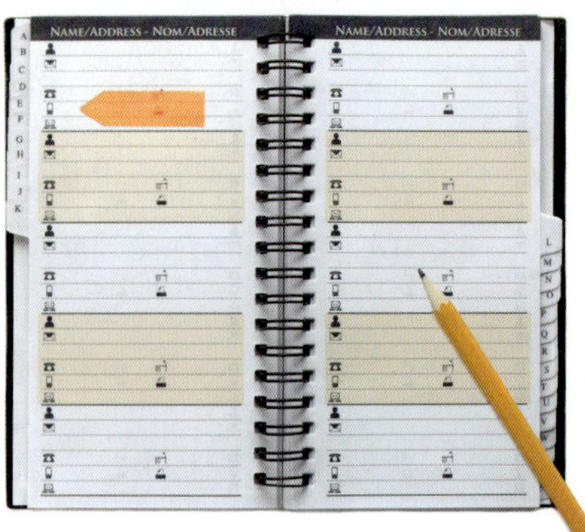

2. What is Mike going to do tonight?
   (A) Go on a date
   (B) Play in a concert
   (C) Meet Susan
   (D) Go for a run

3. Which of the following will the man NOT do over the next two weeks?
   (A) Go to a picnic
   (B) Take a math exam
   (C) Spend time with family
   (D) Take a vacation

4. What is the man worried about?
   (A) He doesn't think his mom can go to the picnic.
   (B) He won't have enough time to study.
   (C) He thinks he will do badly on his English exam.
   (D) He thinks the food will be bad at the picnic.

5. Why is Tracey making this phone call?
   (A) To cancel an appointment
   (B) To invite the man on a date
   (C) To offer the man a job
   (D) To buy tickets for an event

6. When will Tracey see Dr. Morton?
   (A) At 2:30 tomorrow
   (B) At 2:30 today
   (C) At 3:00 today
   (D) At 3:00 tomorrow

DICTATION 1 TRACK 080

A Listen and fill in the blanks.

1. I was ________ to play ____________ ________ at my friend's ________, but my ________ says I have to visit my ________________.
2. I ____________ a soccer game with my ____________, but it is pouring ________, so we can't ________.
3. I ____________ to go to a ________ with my ________, but I have a terrible ____________.
4. I arranged to ________ today ________, but my ________ wants me to finish an ____________ report instead.
5. I lost my ____________, so I can't pay for my ________ ____________ to the ________. I'll have to stay at ________.

B Listen and fill in the blanks.

W Hi, Mike. What's up? I'm ____________ to see if you ________ to ________ a movie or ____________.

M Hi, Susan. I'm just getting ________ to go out.

W Do you ________ a ________ tonight?

M Yes. I'm going to a ____________ with Blake. ____________? We're going to see Allie Felix at the ____________ Arena.

W Oh, ________. That's ____________? Well, I'd ____________ let you ____________ getting ready.

M Yeah, I'm ____________ a little ________.

W OK. ________ me a ________ tomorrow, and we can ________ ________ for next ________. I hope you have a ________ ________ tonight.

C Listen and fill in the blanks.

I ________ it were the ____________ vacation already. But I have ____________ for ________ more weeks. I have a ________ ________ on Tuesday, an ____________ exam on ________________, and a ____________ exam the week after. But I can't ________ much this weekend because it's my mom's ____________ and she wants the whole ____________ to go on a big ____________. It will be ________, but I really need to ________. I think I will ________ ________ on my ____________ exam, but I'm not very ________ ________ math and ________________.

LISTENING TEST

Listen and choose the correct answer.

1. Where will the man go tomorrow morning?

   (A) To the woman's house (B) To a picnic
   (C) To church (D) To school

2. What does the woman tell the man to bring with him?

   (A) A book (B) Nothing
   (C) Something to eat (D) Something to drink

3. Who is making food for the man's party?

   (A) The woman (B) His friends
   (C) The man (D) The man's mother

4. Why does the woman think the man should pay for movie tickets?

   (A) Because she wants to see a movie
   (B) To say thank you to his mom
   (C) Because he rarely pays for anything
   (D) To help give the theater more business

5. Why isn't the woman free tonight?

   (A) She has to study.
   (B) She has to play sport.
   (C) She has to help the man.
   (D) She is feeling bad.

6. What will the speakers do next week?

   (A) Take an exam
   (B) Play baseball
   (C) Watch sports together
   (D) Study together

DICTATION 2

A Listen and fill in the blanks.

W Are you ________ to the ________ tomorrow?
M I'll ______ to go. But I'm not ______ yet if I can ______ it.
W Why's that?
M I have ________ until ______.
W That's ______ a ________. It doesn't really ______ until ______.
M In that case, I ______ I can go.
W ______ anytime. It'll go until ______.
M Should I ______ something to ______ or ______?
W No, just ______ ________!

B Listen and fill in the blanks.

W Hi, Joe. I'm ________ about your ______ tomorrow. What ______ should I ______?
M ______ to my ____________ any time ______ ______.
W Sounds ______. Have you ________ food for the ______?
M Yes, my ______ and her ________ are going to ______.
W That's ______ of them. Is your ______ coming to the ______?
M No, she ______ she'd bring the food, then she's ______ to a ______ with her ________.
W I hope you are ________ for their ________.
M Hey, that's a ______ ______. What a great ______ ______ gift!

C Listen and fill in the blanks.

M Are you ______ this ________?
W No, I ______ to ______ for a ______ exam tonight.
M That's too ______. Well, do you ______ any help ________? You ______ that I'm ________ good at math.
W No, that's ______. I study ________ ______.
M How ______ going to a ________ ______ next ______?
W ______ sounds like ______. I'll have ________ of time next ______.
M ______. I'll ______ the days and ______ of the ______.

In the Kitchen

KEY WORDS

Listen for these words and phrases.

burn	oven	show	mix	recipe
turn on/off	chop	boil	pasta	stir

KEY EXPRESSIONS

TRACK 084

Listen and match each question with its correct answer.

1. Is spaghetti difficult to make? •
2. Could you teach me how to make French food? •
3. How long should I put this in the oven for? •
4. Are these carrots small enough? •
5. What's that smell? •

• (A) No, you need to chop them into tiny pieces.
• (B) Twenty minutes should be long enough.
• (C) I think the pizza is burning.
• (D) No, it's very easy.
• (E) Of course. I'll teach you my favorite dish.

WARM-UP

Listen and check what the speaker is making.

1. (A) A sandwich (B) Bread
2. (A) Soup (B) A cake
3. (A) Pasta (B) Toast
4. (A) Boiled eggs (B) Fried eggs
5. (A) Pizza (B) Salad

LISTEN FOR IT

Listen and check what the speaker needs to do.

1. (A) Chop vegetables (B) Boil vegetables
2. (A) Turn on the heat (B) Turn off the heat
3. (A) Write a recipe (B) Find a recipe
4. (A) Buy tomatoes (B) Buy a pizza
5. (A) Put bread in the oven (B) Take bread out of the oven

TRUE OR FALSE

Listen and write T for true or F for false.

1. _______ (A) The boy's father is not a very good cook.
   _______ (B) The boy likes spaghetti.

2. _______ (A) The woman uses recipes that she finds on the internet.
   _______ (B) The woman enjoyed beef with blueberries.

3. _______ (A) The woman's husband does all of the cooking.
   _______ (B) The woman works in an office.

LISTENING PRACTICE

Listen and choose the correct answer.

1. What does the man want to learn?

   (A) How to cook spaghetti with sauce
   (B) How to cook pasta without sauce
   (C) How to make sauce only
   (D) How to eat spaghetti

2. What problem do the man and woman have?

   (A) They don't know how to cook.
   (B) They don't have any spaghetti.
   (C) Their pot is too small.
   (D) They don't have much time today.

3. Why does the man think it is better to make your own pizza?

   (A) It tastes better.
   (B) It's quicker.
   (C) It's cheaper.
   (D) It looks better.

4. Why is the man going to eat salad?

   (A) Because he doesn't like pizza
   (B) Because the pizza is burned
   (C) Because he isn't hungry
   (D) Because he had pizza yesterday

5. How long should the woman leave the food in the oven?

   (A) A couple of minutes
   (B) Twenty minutes
   (C) Twenty-five minutes
   (D) One hour

6. Which of the following is NOT true about the dish they are making?

   (A) It includes carrots.
   (B) It has a sauce.
   (C) It has onions in it.
   (D) It includes cheese.

DICTATION 1

A Listen and fill in the blanks.

1. All these ________________ are very ________. I have to ________ them ________.
2. Oh, no! The ________ is ____________. I need to turn off the ________.
3. I can't ____________ how to make my grandmother's ________ ________. I need a ____________.
4. I need ________ ____________ for this pizza, but I only have ________. I need to go to the ________.
5. The ________ is ____________. I'd better take it out of the ________.

B Listen and fill in the blanks.

M Is spaghetti ______________ to ________?
W No, it's very ________.
M Could you ________ me how to ________ it?
W Well, do you just ________ to ________ how to cook ________, or do you want to ________ how to make a ________ as well?
M Oh, I ________ I need a sauce, too.
W I ________ so. Give me that ________ ________ so I can ________ some water, and we can get ____________.
M ________. I need to ________ something.
W ________? Don't ________ me that we don't have any ________________.
M That's ________.
W I'll ________ you ____________ day.

C Listen and fill in the blanks.

W It was a ________ idea to make ________ together. It was ________!
M Yes. It's much ____________ to make your ________ pizza because it's ____________ than ____________ it.
W What's that ________?
M Oh, no. I think the ________ is ____________. Didn't you ________ ________ the oven?
W No, I left it ________ to ________ the pizza ________.
M And now it's ________.
W It's ________. We can still ________ it. Actually, it ________ and ________ really good. It's making me ____________, just ____________ at it.
M I ________ I'll have a ________ instead.

LISTENING TEST

Listen and choose the correct answer.

1. What is Pierre going to teach the woman?
   (A) How to make food from his home country
   (B) Where to find good French food
   (C) The name of his favorite food
   (D) How to speak French

2. What cooking technique does Pierre NOT mention?
   (A) Fry
   (B) Boil
   (C) Chop
   (D) Stir

3. What does the boy offer to do?
   (A) Cook chicken
   (B) Stir something
   (C) Chop vegetables
   (D) Make soup

4. Why is the woman surprised?
   (A) The boy made dinner for her.
   (B) The boy said the soup smells bad.
   (C) The boy came home early.
   (D) The boy ate all the soup.

5. What is the woman mainly talking about?
   (A) Her favorite cooking show
   (B) Where to buy spices
   (C) Why she hates cooking shows
   (D) Her favorite chef

6. What will the woman eat for her dinner?
   (A) A dish she saw on TV
   (B) A new recipe she wants to try
   (C) Chinese food
   (D) Pizza

DICTATION 2 TRACK 091

A Listen and fill in the blanks.

W Pierre, you're from ________, aren't ________?

M ________, I grew up near ________.

W ________ you ________ me how to make ________ food?

M Of ________. I'll ________ you my ________ ________. I love cooking. It will be ________ to ________ you. I hope you like ________, because my favorite ________ is a ________ stew.

W Oh, yes. I like beef ________ ________. Is this a ________ dish?

W Not at all. You ________ the meat and ________, put them in a ________ with some ________ and salt, ________ it all and then ________.

M That ________ very easy.

B Listen and fill in the blanks.

M ________, do you ________ me to ________ this soup?

W Yes, ________. That would be very ________. I don't want it to ________.

M OK. It doesn't ________ very ________. What's in it?

W What do you ________ it doesn't ________ good? You ________ this soup. It's my ________ ________.

M Oh, but it looks ________ today.

W Well, that's ________ because I didn't put the ________ in ________.

M ________ you put the ________ in ________?

W No, not ________. When did you ________ the ________ expert?

M I saw a ________ ________ on TV. The ________ put in the ________ first.

C Listen and fill in the blanks.

I don't ________ to watch ________ ________ on TV. ________ chefs and ________ say things like "You don't ________ to buy anything ________ to make this ________." But they ________ use a ________ or vegetable that I don't ________. They ________, "This will take ________ ________ to make." ________ it takes me an ________. They say, "This ________ looks ________." But it looks ________ when I make it. Cooking shows don't ________ ________ ________. Cooking is ________ and ________. I think I'll ________ a pizza ________.

What's Wrong?

KEY WORDS

Listen for these words and phrases.

cough	cold	headache	sore throat	fever
bruise	medicine	scratch	food poisoning	injection

KEY EXPRESSIONS

Listen and match each question with its correct answer.

1. Do you get enough sleep?	(A) I have a cold.
2. What's wrong with you?	(B) No, I've always been very healthy.
3. Have you ever stayed in the hospital?	(C) I fell off my bike and hit my head.
4. Are you taking any medicine?	(D) Not really. I have trouble falling asleep.
5. How did you get that bruise?	(E) Yes, I took some a couple of hours ago.

WARM-UP

TRACK 094

Listen and check what is wrong with the speaker.

1. (A) Fever (B) Sore throat
2. (A) Cut hand (B) Food poisoning
3. (A) Cold (B) Bruise
4. (A) Headache (B) Stomachache
5. (A) Food poisoning (B) Cough

LISTEN FOR IT

TRACK 095

Listen and check why the speaker went to the hospital.

1. (A) To see her sick daughter (B) To see her new grandchild
2. (A) Because he has a sore throat (B) Because he has a sore head
3. (A) To get an injection (B) To get some pills
4. (A) Because he fell from a tree (B) Because he has a fever
5. (A) Because she has a bad bruise (B) Because she has a bad scratch

TRUE OR FALSE

TRACK 096

Listen and write T for true or F for false.

1. _______ (A) Winston's is a medicine for people with a cold.
   _______ (B) Winston's has a lemon flavor.

2. _______ (A) The man got medicine from his doctor.
   _______ (B) The man needs to do less exercise.

3. _______ (A) The girl had a high fever.
   _______ (B) Vickie will come home in a few days.

LISTENING PRACTICE

Listen and choose the correct answer.

1. What is the man's problem?

   (A) He has a headache.
   (B) He has a fever.
   (C) He can't sleep well.
   (D) He sleeps too much.

2. What is the doctor's advice?

   (A) Try to sleep more
   (B) Find a new job
   (C) Take medicine
   (D) Do yoga

3. Why did the man need to go to the hospital when he was younger?

   (A) He had a bad fever.
   (B) He broke his leg.
   (C) He broke his arm.
   (D) He hurt his head.

4. Which of the following is NOT something that the man remembers about staying in the hospital?

   (A) Eating candy
   (B) Missing school
   (C) Playing computer games
   (D) Watching movies

5. Which of the following does the man NOT have?

   (A) A headache
   (B) A cough
   (C) A sore throat
   (D) A fever

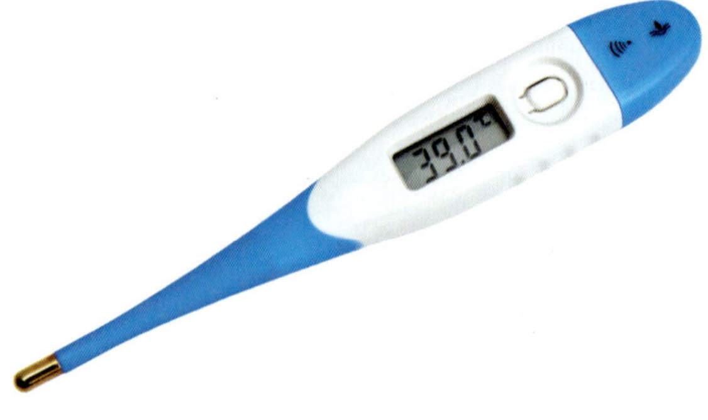

6. What is the woman going to do?

   (A) Call a doctor
   (B) Buy medicine for the man
   (C) Take a day off work
   (D) Go to work at the pharmacy

A Listen and fill in the blanks.

1. My ________ had her first ________ yesterday. Now I'm a ________. I went to see the ________ this ________!
2. I had a ________ car accident ________, and now my ________ really hurts.
3. I'm going to ________ in Africa this ________, and I ________ to get some ________ first.
4. I ________ out of a ________ in our yard. I have a big ________ on my head, so ________ thinks I should ________ a ________.
5. My cat ________ me, and now my whole ________ is ________ and ________.

B Listen and fill in the blanks.

W ________, Mr. Anderson. What ________ to be the ________?
M I'm so ________ all the ________.
W ________ you get enough ________?
M Not ________. I have trouble ________ ________.
W When did this ________?
M ________ a ________ ago.
W Are you ________ about ________?
M Well, I ________ my ________, and now I am ________. I am very ________ about finding a ________ job.
W I'm ________ to hear that. I ________ doing yoga to ________ before you go to ________.

C Listen and fill in the blanks.

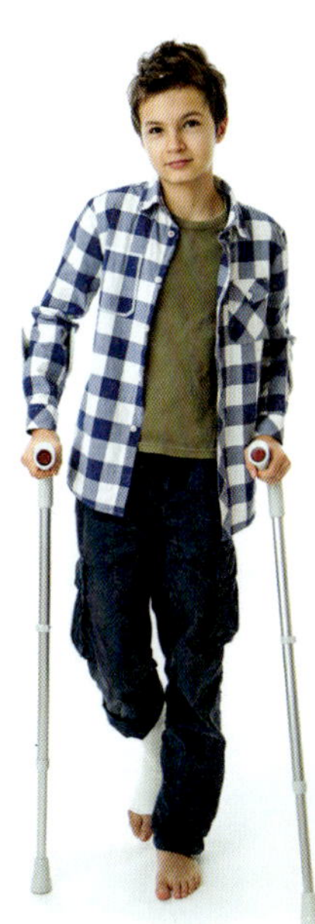

M ________ you ever ________ in the ________, Tina?
W No, I've ________ been very ________. How about you?
M ________. When I was ________ years old, I spent ________ days in the ________.
W ________ days? What ________?
M I fell ________ the ________ in our house, and I ________ my ________.
W Did it ________ a lot?
M ________, but I don't ________ much about it. ________ I remember is that I ________ ________ to go to ________ and my ________ let me eat ________ and watch movies!
W And your ________ is ________ now?
M Oh, ________. I have ________ strong ________ now.

LISTENING TEST

TRACK 099

Listen and choose the correct answer.

1. What does the woman want to do?

   (A) Leave work early
   (B) Take a sick day
   (C) Take a vacation
   (D) Come to work late

2. Why does the woman need injections?

   (A) She is sick.
   (B) She doesn't say why.
   (C) She is going to travel to countries where she might get sick.
   (D) She just came back from countries where there are serious diseases.

3. What is wrong with the woman?

   (A) She hurt her leg.
   (B) She hurt her head.
   (C) She has a cold.
   (D) She has a fever.

4. What does the man think the woman should do?

   (A) Take some medicine
   (B) Get some rest
   (C) Go to bed
   (D) See a doctor

5. What probably gave the woman a stomachache?

   (A) Bread
   (B) Jam
   (C) An apple
   (D) Fish

6. What does the man suggest?

   (A) Eat more bread
   (B) Complain to the restaurant
   (C) Drink water
   (D) Nothing

A Listen and fill in the blanks.

W Can I _______ work a little _______ today? I have a doctor's _______________.

M Yes, that's _______. I hope _______________ is OK.

W Oh, I'm not _______. I _______ to get a couple of _______________.

M _______ is that?

W I'm going to ___________ in some _______________ where I could get a ___________ disease. The _______________ will help keep me ___________.

M Which _______________ will you visit?

W Well, _______ I'll go to Kenya, _______ I'll _______ _______ Malawi.

M That ___________ like an _______________ trip. I hope the _______________ don't hurt too _______.

B Listen and fill in the blanks.

M Are you _______? You don't _______ so good. Are you _______?

W My _______ hurts.

M How did you get that ___________?

W I fell off my _______ and _______ my _______.

M I _______ you should see a ___________.

W No, I'm OK.

M _______ you taking any ___________?

W Yes, I _______ some a couple of _______ ago.

M _______ it help _______ the _______?

W Not ___________. Maybe I will _______ the ___________ after all.

C Listen and fill in the blanks.

W I have a ___________.

M _______ you eat something ___________?

W No, I had _______ with _______ for breakfast. I ate an _______. Oh, but I had _______ for _______, and it tasted very strange.

M _______ you have _______ ___________.

W It did _______ a bit _______. But I don't ___________ like _______, so I thought it was ___________.

M Well, _______ lots of _______. Don't _______ anything else today.

W No ___________. I'm not at all ___________ anyway.

Unit 12 Recycle!

KEY WORDS

Listen for these words and phrases.

reuse	recycle	trash can	waste	save
glass	plastic	Earth	separate	can

KEY EXPRESSIONS

Listen and match each question with its correct answer.

1. Do you need a bag?
2. Do you recycle paper?
3. Can I put this glass bottle in the trash can?
4. Why is it important to recycle?
5. What's this box made of?

(A) No, you need to separate the trash.
(B) It's a good way to reduce waste.
(C) Yes, I always recycle it.
(D) No, thanks. I brought my own.
(E) It looks like plastic to me.

WARM-UP (Track 103)

Listen and check what the speaker needs to recycle.

1. (A) New paper (B) Newspaper
2. (A) Soda can (B) Soup can
3. (A) Plastic (B) Glass
4. (A) Plastic bottles (B) Cans
5. (A) Paper bags (B) Plastic bags

LISTEN FOR IT

Listen and check what the speaker never buys.

1. (A) Vegetables (B) Large bags of food
2. (A) Glass bottles (B) Plastic bottles
3. (A) New baby clothes (B) Baby toys
4. (A) Newspapers (B) Paper for wrapping gifts
5. (A) Plastic toys (B) Children's clothes

TRUE OR FALSE

Listen and write T for true or F for false.

1. ______ (A) You can buy a plastic bag for 10 cents.
   ______ (B) The woman has her own shopping bag.

2. ______ (A) The man doesn't like to recycle.
   ______ (B) The man sometimes buys a newspaper.

3. ______ (A) The girl hates to separate trash.
   ______ (B) The girl has to put paper in a yellow box.

LISTENING PRACTICE

Listen and choose the correct answer.

1. Why does the man tell his daughter to put the newspapers in the trash can?
   (A) He is not worried about recycling.
   (B) He was not listening to her question.
   (C) He doesn't know where the papers should go.
   (D) He wants them to go in the trash.

2. Why can't the girl put the papers in the recycling container?
   (A) She can't find it.
   (B) They don't have one.
   (C) It is too full.
   (D) She is too short.

3. What does the woman want to know?
   (A) Whether the box has any symbols
   (B) Whether the man has the box
   (C) Whether the box can be reused
   (D) Whether the box can be recycled

4. What interesting information does the woman learn?
   (A) Where to recycle plastic boxes
   (B) The meaning of a symbol
   (C) The cost of making plastic
   (D) How to make a triangle

5. Where is this conversation taking place?
   (A) At the woman's home
   (B) At a supermarket
   (C) At a school
   (D) On a bus

6. What problem does the man have?
   (A) It's difficult to remember his shopping bag.
   (B) He doesn't know where to buy a shopping bag.
   (C) He hates shopping.
   (D) Food is too expensive.

DICTATION 1

A Listen and fill in the blanks.

1. I live _______ and I don't like to _______ food, so I never _______ large bags of _______________.
2. ___________ is not ___________, so I never buy drinks in ___________ bottles.
3. I don't buy _______ clothes for my _______. I buy _______ clothes, then I will _______ them to another ___________ when he gets _______.
4. I don't buy _______ to wrap ___________ presents. I _______ them in _______________!
5. I _______ buy ___________ toys for my ___________. In fact, I _______ a lot of _______ myself.

B Listen and fill in the blanks.

W Dad, _______ can I put these _______________?

M You can _______ them in the _______ _______.

W _______! I can't just _______ them _______.

M Oh, _______. I wasn't _______________ properly. _______ don't you put them in the _______________ _______________? That's where _______ should go.

W Because it's _______, there is no _______.

M OK, _______ put them on the _______ next to the _______________. I'll take them to the _______________ center _______.

C Listen and fill in the blanks.

W What's this _______ _______ of?

M It _______ like ___________ to me.

W Yes, I was thinking the same _______. Do you _______ I can ___________ it?

M _______ it have _______ symbols on it? _______ there is a symbol that _______ you if _______________ can be ___________.

W _______ idea. I'll _______... OK, it says PET, and it has a ___________ _______ in a ___________. What does that _______?

M We have a _______ on the _______. Let's have a _______.

W Right. Good _______. This one is _______ for _______________. That's useful _______________. I will try to ___________ those ___________ and the ___________.

LISTENING TEST

Listen and choose the correct answer.

1. What does the man want to do?
   (A) Throw away all his trash in one place
   (B) Recycle his glass bottle
   (C) Move to a bigger apartment
   (D) Buy some boxes

2. What does the woman suggest that the man do?
   (A) Recycle paper
   (B) Use a plastic box
   (C) Buy more glass and cans
   (D) Reduce how much trash he makes

3. What is the conversation mainly about?
   (A) How to recycle paper
   (B) What kinds of paper to recycle
   (C) Things you can make with paper
   (D) Where to buy recycled paper

4. Which is NOT something that people make with old paper?
   (A) Bowls
   (B) Beds
   (C) Bags
   (D) Beads

5. What does the boy want to know?
   (A) The reason why people recycle
   (B) The reason why his mom drives a truck
   (C) The reason why trash is bad for Earth
   (D) The reason why people make trash

6. How does the boy feel about trash?
   (A) Excited
   (B) Interested
   (C) Sad
   (D) Pleased

DICTATION 2

A Listen and fill in the blanks.

M _______ I put this _______ bottle in the _______ _______?

W No, you need to _________ the _______. Everyone who _______ in the _________ building has to _________ their _______ first.

M But _______ _______ will know if I _________.

W But you _______ to live on _______, don't you? You know it's __________ to recycle. Help _______ _______!

M OK, I'll get a _______ for glass _________ to keep in my _________.

W You'd better get boxes for _______, _______, and _________ as well. They all need to be __________.

M But my __________ is too _______.

W Then you _______ to make _______ _______!

B Listen and fill in the blanks.

W Do you _________ _______?

M Of _________. And I try to _______ recycled _______ whenever I can. _______ about you?

W Yeah, me too. I _______ something _________ about things _________ do with _______ paper. It was cool to _______ different _______ to _________ paper.

M _______ kinds of _________?

W I saw a _______ made of old _______, and _______ bags made of magazine _______.

M Oh, I've seen _______ beads. You _______ the paper into a little _______, then _______ it. You can _______ a necklace.

W That _________ like a _______ thing to do. I might _______ that with my _________.

C Listen and fill in the blanks.

M Mom, I have a _________.
Why is it __________ to _________?

W It's a _______ way to _________ _______.

M What _________ if we don't _________?

W Well, _______ do you think all the _______ goes?

M A _______ takes it _______. But I don't know _______ the truck _______.

W It _______ to a landfill—that's a _______ where _______ is put into the _________.
And it _______ there, well, _________.

M It just _______ there?

W _______. Forever. It's bad for _______, it _________ bad, and it looks _______.

M Yuck. That makes me _______ _______. I don't want to make any _______.

Transcripts

Unit 1 At the Office

KEY WORDS Track 002

Listen for these words and phrases.

meeting	presentation
stationery	appointment
printer	copier
client	report
sick day	business card

KEY EXPRESSIONS Track 003

Listen and match each question with its correct answer.

1. Do you have any idea what's wrong with the printer?
2. I'm afraid I need to use a sick day today.
3. Could I have your business card?
4. Have you finished the sales report yet?
5. Who should I see about ordering ink?

WARM-UP Track 004

Listen and check what the speaker has to do today.

1. I have to submit this report to my boss by five o'clock, so I really need to finish writing it.
2. My child has a fever, so I need to stay home today and look after her.
3. I have an appointment with an important client at two o'clock today.
4. My computer seems to be having some problems, so I must make copies of all my files.
5. I finally finished the report for the meeting. Now I need to print off twenty copies.

LISTEN FOR IT Track 005

Listen and check the correct situation.

1. If you look at this, you can see that sales are up this month.
2. Thank you for coming, Miss Penney. I see that you have a lot of experience in this type of work.
3. I'd like three packs of paper and four packs of printer ink. Can you deliver them by Friday?
4. OK, it looks like everyone is here. So, the first thing to discuss is the Leeman project.
5. Which button do I press to make the size bigger?

TRUE OR FALSE Track 006

Listen and write T for true or F for false.

1. **W** I work for the sales division of my company. I have to give a lot of presentations in my job. I used to feel very nervous, but not now. I simply make sure I practice what I want to say at least three times.
2. **M** I always carry business cards with me. It looks more professional if I can give someone a card with my company name and logo and my contact details.
3. **W** I used to write all my appointments in a day planner, but now I simply put them in the calendar on my phone. However, last week I lost my phone, and I didn't know when any of my appointments were!

LISTENING PRACTICE Track 007

Listen and choose the correct answer.

Questions 1 and 2 refer to the following dialog.

M Do you have any idea what's wrong with the printer? I can't get it to work.
W It might be out of paper.
M That's what I thought. But I checked, and there is plenty of paper.
W Is it switched off? Or perhaps there's no ink?
M That's it. The black ink has run out.
W Oh, and there isn't a spare ink in the cupboard.
M Who should I see about ordering ink?
W Marina is in charge of stationery supplies.
M Got it.

Questions 3 and 4 refer to the following dialog.

W Mark, have you finished the sales report yet?
M Almost. I'll have it on your desk by the end of the day.
W Actually, you can give it to me tomorrow afternoon. I have some new details. You'll have to change a lot of the numbers for the new office building.
M Oh, no. It looks like I'll be working late tonight then.
W Yes, sorry about that. But I really appreciate your hard work.
M At least it's Friday tomorrow.

Questions 5 and 6 refer to the following talk.

W Most days, I have a lot of meetings. Some of these meetings are with my coworkers and the rest are with clients. I think most meetings are much longer than necessary. Some of my coworkers like to keep talking about the same issue, even when we have already made a decision. They won't stop talking about it.

It wastes time. Luckily, most people want to finish meetings quickly. Well, I have to go. I have a meeting and I don't want to be late.

DICTATION 1 Track 008

A. Listen and fill in the blanks.

1. If you look at this, you can see that sales are up this month.
2. Thank you for coming, Miss Penney. I see that you have a lot of experience in this type of work.
3. I'd like three packs of paper and four packs of printer ink. Can you deliver them by Friday?
4. OK, it looks like everyone is here. So, the first thing to discuss is the Leeman project.
5. Which button do I press to make the size bigger?

B. Listen and fill in the blanks.

M Do you have any idea what's wrong with the printer? I can't get it to work.
W It might be out of paper.
M That's what I thought. But I checked, and there is plenty of paper.
W Is it switched off? Or perhaps there's no ink?
M That's it. The black ink has run out.
W Oh, and there isn't a spare ink in the cupboard.
M Who should I see about ordering ink?
W Marina is in charge of stationery supplies.
M Got it.

C. Listen and fill in the blanks.

W Mark, have you finished the sales report yet?
M Almost. I'll have it on your desk by the end of the day.
W Actually, You can give it to me tomorrow afternoon. I have some new details. You'll have to change a lot of the numbers for the new office building.
M Oh, no. It looks like I'll be working late tonight then.
W Yes, sorry about that. But I really appreciate your hard work.
M At least it's Friday tomorrow.

LISTENING TEST Track 009

Listen and choose the correct answer.

Questions 1 and 2 refer to the following dialog.

W I really enjoyed your presentation. In your workplace, do you do all the things that you described?
M In fact, I do. Since we started using the five step process, all of our staff are much happier. And their work is better.
W Wow. I'd love to know more about how that works. I'd like to make some changes at the company where I work, but I don't really know where to start.
M Well, I'd be happy to answer any questions.
W Could I have your business card?
M Sure. It has my office number and work email address.
W Thank you.

Questions 3 and 4 refer to the following dialog.

M Hello? Amy?
W Yes. Is that Patrick? You don't sound very good.
M No, I feel terrible. I'm afraid I need to use a sick day today.
W OK, well I hope you feel better tomorrow. Is there anything that needs to be done today?
M Well, if you have time. I left a pile of documents by the copier. I was going to copy them and then give the copies to everyone on the finance team. You couldn't ask Tim to do that for me, could you?
W Sure. And I'll ask him to leave the originals on your desk.
M Thank you so much.

Questions 5 and 6 refer to the following dialog.

M We've run out of paper and pens again! The stationery was delivered just a couple of days ago.
W I know. It's becoming a problem. I think people are taking things home.
M I agree. I think we need to ask the staff to fill in a form each time they take an item of stationery.
W Yes. If they have to sign a form, they will be less likely to take extra things.
M OK, well, I will mention it at the next meeting. I'm sure plenty of people will complain, but I think it's necessary.
W Great. Well, I support you in this decision.

DICTATION 2 Track 010

A. Listen and fill in the blanks.

W I really enjoyed your presentation. In your workplace, do you do all the things that you described?

M In fact, I do. Since we started using the five-step process, all of our staff are much happier. And their work is better.

W Wow. I'd love to know more about how that works. I'd like to make some changes at the company where I work, but I don't really know where to start.

M Well, I'd be happy to answer any questions.

W Could I have your business card?

M Sure. It has my office number and work email address.

W Thank you.

B. Listen and fill in the blanks.

M Hello? Amy?

W Yes. Is that Patrick? You don't sound very good.

M No, I feel terrible. I'm afraid I need to use a sick day today.

W OK, well I hope you feel better tomorrow. Is there anything that needs to be done today?

M Well, if you have time. I left a pile of documents by the copier. I was going to copy them and then give the copies to everyone on the finance team. You couldn't ask Tim to do that for me, could you?

W Sure. And I'll ask him to leave the originals on your desk.

M Thank you so much.

C. Listen and fill in the blanks.

M We've run out of paper and pens again! The stationery was delivered just a couple of days ago.

W I know. It's becoming a problem. I think people are taking things home.

M I agree. I think we need to ask the staff to fill in a form each time they take an item of stationery.

W Yes. If they have to sign a form, they will be less likely to take extra things.

M OK, well, I will mention it at the next meeting. I'm sure plenty of people will complain, but I think it's necessary.

W Great. Well, I support you in this decision.

Unit 2 On Time

KEY WORDS Track 011

Listen for these words and phrases.

calendar	month
anniversary	schedule
ago	ahead of time
postpone	later
while	promptly

KEY EXPRESSIONS Track 012

Listen and match each question with its correct answer.

1. Look at the time. It's already a quarter to one.
2. Is the bus often late?
3. How much longer until we land in Singapore?
4. Has the 3:00 bus already come?
5. What time do you begin work?

WARM-UP Track 013

Listen and check what times the business is open.

1. Thank you for calling the Branson Public Library. Our hours are Monday to Friday 8:30 - 6:00. We are closed on weekends and public holidays.
2. Save Mart thanks you for your call. We are currently closed for business. Our daily business hours are 6:30 a.m. to 11:00 p.m. We hope you will drop by to take advantage of some of our weekly specials.
3. You have reached the offices of Midway Airlines. Our offices are closed at this time. Office hours are from 9 a.m. to 6 p.m. Monday to Friday and 9 a.m. to noon on Saturdays. We are closed on Sundays.
4. My local store opens at 6:30, so I usually buy my lunch on the way to work. It closes at 8:00 p.m., so I often buy vegetables on my way home.
5. I can't believe it. The library changed its hours. It closes at 3:00 p.m. on Wednesdays. It used to close at 5:00. I should have come at 10:00 when it opened.

LISTEN FOR IT Track 014

Listen and check where the speaker has to be at a certain time.

1. School starts at 9:00, but it takes 45 minutes to get there by bus. I need to be at the bus stop at 8:05 if I want to get to school on time.

2. According to the train schedule, the last train to Baker Street leaves at 11:45. It's already 11:35, so I'll have to run!
3. It's my parents' 20th wedding anniversary. I have to be at their house by 3:30 to decorate their house for a surprise party!
4. I have an interview for an office job at 11:00. I have to arrive twenty minutes before the time of the interview.
5. My mom shouted at me for coming home late after school last night, so I have to be home by 5:00 every day from now on.

TRUE OR FALSE Track 015

Listen and write T for true or F for false.

1. **W** I'm going to watch a movie with my friend Lisa. *Love Kills* is showing at 2, 5, and 8 o'clock. But *On Our Own* is showing at 2, 3 and 7 o'clock. I don't want to get home too late, so I hope Lisa agrees to watch *Love Kills*.
2. **M** Welcome aboard the Airport Limousine Bus. Buses leave from the airport to the downtown hotel every 20 minutes. This bus will leave at 2:30 promptly. The ride will take roughly one hour. Tickets will be collected from the driver at your destination. In the meantime, sit back and enjoy the ride.
3. **W** Welcome to the first day of our conference. Our first speaker will speak from 8:30 to 9:45. We'll then have a coffee break until 10:00. We'll continue with our panel discussion at 10:00. Feel free to bring your drink with you if it helps you get back on time.

LISTENING PRACTICE Track 016

Listen and choose the correct answer.

Questions 1 and 2 refer to the following dialog.

M Look at the time! It's already a quarter to one.
W Really? How time flies. It's almost time to get back to the office. Why does lunch time always go by so quickly?
M I know. I'd better hurry and finish my lunch. I think I'll get a doggy bag for the rest of this spaghetti. It's too good to leave.
W We got here at twelve, but it seems like only a few minutes.
M I know. Let's call the waitress and get the check.
W Put your wallet away. It's my treat. It is your birthday after all!

Questions 3 and 4 refer to the following dialog.

M How much longer until we land in Singapore?
W About six and a half hours.
M That's still so long. I'm getting bored now.
W You'll just have to read your book or watch another movie. I'm going to try to get some sleep. And besides, the pilot said that we will arrive ahead of schedule.
M I guess that's a good thing.
W Well, it's a lot better than arriving behind schedule. Last time I traveled by airplane, we left two hours late!

Questions 5 and 6 refer to the following dialog.

M Excuse me. Do you have the time?
W Sure, it's 3:05.
M Has the 3:00 bus already come?
W I don't think so. I've been waiting here since 2:45. But I'm not sure what time the bus is supposed to come.
M Oh good. This bus only comes every thirty minutes.
W Is the bus always late?
M No, it's usually on time. But if the traffic is bad, it can be a little late. It's usually pretty good at this time of day, but the four o'clock bus is often late. The local schools end at four, so there are a lot of parents' cars on the road at that time.

DICTATION 1 Track 017

A. Listen and fill in the blanks.

1. School starts at 9:00, but it takes 45 minutes to get there by bus. I need to be at the bus stop at 8:05 if I want to get to school on time.
2. According to the train schedule, the last train to Baker Street leaves at 11:45. It's already 11:35, so I'll have to run!
3. It's my parents' 20th wedding anniversary. I have to be at their house by 3:30 to decorate their house for a surprise party!
4. I have an interview for an office job at 11:00. I have to arrive twenty minutes before the time of the interview.
5. My mom shouted at me for coming home late after school last night, so I have to be home by 5:00 every day from now on.

B. Listen and fill in the blanks.

M Look at the time! It's already a quarter to one.

W Really? How time flies. It's almost time to get back to the office. Why does lunch time always go by so quickly?

M I know. I'd better hurry and finish my lunch. I think I'll get a doggy bag for the rest of this spaghetti. It's too good to leave.

W We got here at twelve, but it seems like only a few minutes.

M I know. Let's call the waitress and get the check.

W Put your wallet away. It's my treat. It is your birthday after all!

C. Listen and fill in the blanks.

M How much longer until we land in Singapore?

W About six and a half hours.

M That's still so long. I'm getting bored now.

W You'll just have to read your book or watch another movie. I'm going to try to get some sleep. And besides, the pilot said that we will arrive ahead of schedule.

M I guess that's a good thing.

W Well, it's a lot better than arriving behind schedule. Last time I traveled by airplane, we left two hours late!

LISTENING TEST Track 018

Listen and choose the correct answer.

Questions 1 and 2 refer to the following dialog.

M What time do you begin work?

W I start work at 10:30 every morning. I like that I don't start very early.

M How late do you usually work?

W 6:00. On Fridays I sometimes work until 8:00 because the store stays open later.

M Do you ever work on Saturday?

W Yes, I sometimes put in a half day.

M What's your busiest month?

W December. It's because of the Christmas season. While everyone is out shopping, I'm working hard!

Questions 3 and 4 refer to the following dialog.

W Aren't we going to the neighborhood meeting tonight? It's almost time to leave. Why are you making popcorn?

M No, they postponed the meeting until next week.

W Oh, so when is the meeting now?

M It's not until next Thursday at 7:00.

W How long have you known that?

M Brian phoned me a few hours ago to let me know.

W I really wish you had told me ahead of time. It's really annoying. I hurried home from work. I could have finished my reports instead.

M I'm sorry. I'll mark it on the calendar so we don't forget.

Questions 5 and 6 refer to the following dialog.

M I'd like to see Dr. Wilson, please.

W Do you have an appointment?

M My appointment was at 3:30.

W It's nearly 5:00, sir. The doctor is with his last patient of the day.

M I know, but I got stuck in traffic. Can I see him first thing in the morning?

W Hmm. Let me see… Yes, he has an opening at 8:30 tomorrow. But if you miss that appointment too, we will have to charge you a fee.

DICTATION 2 Track 019

A. Listen and fill in the blanks.

M What time do you begin work?

W I start work at 10:30 every morning. I like that I don't start very early.

M How late do you usually work?

W 6:00. On Fridays I sometimes work until 8:00 because the store stays open later.

M Do you ever work on Saturday?

W Yes, I sometimes put in a half day.

M What's your busiest month?

W December. It's because of the Christmas season. While everyone is out shopping, I'm working hard!

B. Listen and fill in the blanks.

W Aren't we going to the neighborhood meeting tonight? It's almost time to leave. Why are you making popcorn?

M No, they postponed the meeting until next week.

W Oh, so when is the meeting now?

M It's not until next Thursday at 7:00.

W How long have you known that?

M Brian phoned me a few hours ago to let me know.

W I really wish you had told me ahead of time. It's really annoying. I hurried home from work. I could have finished my reports instead.

M I'm sorry. I'll mark it on the calendar so we don't forget.

C. Listen and fill in the blanks.

M I'd like to see Dr. Wilson, please.
W Do you have an appointment?
M My appointment was at 3:30.
W It's nearly 5:00, sir. The doctor is with his last patient of the day.
M I know, but I got stuck in traffic. Can I see him first thing in the morning?
W Hmm. Let me see... Yes, he has an opening at 8:30 tomorrow. But if you miss that appointment too, we will have to charge you a fee.

Unit 3 Feeling Good

KEY WORDS Track 020

Listen for these words.

confused	pleased
disappointed	frustrated
upset	annoyed
worried	surprised
nervous	embarrassed

KEY EXPRESSIONS Track 021

Listen and match each question with its correct answer.

1. What's wrong?
2. I feel miserable.
3. Do you ever feel frustrated?
4. Are you angry at me?
5. What do you do when you feel lonely?

WARM-UP Track 022

Listen and check how the speaker feels.

1. I didn't study very much for my exam, and I think I got a lot of questions wrong. I am nervous about getting my score.
2. My friends all forgot my birthday today. I didn't get any gifts or cards from anyone.
3. I got a new job! I start next week. It's going to be great!
4. Today I fell over in front of a big group of people. They all laughed at me. It was terrible.
5. My son broke a window, and now I have to pay for it.

LISTEN FOR IT Track 023

Listen and check how the speaker is feeling now.

1. We have to do a big homework assignment, but I didn't understand the instructions that the teacher gave us.
2. My boss wants me to stay late and finish a report, but I promised my wife that we would go to the movies.
3. My grandmother is sick again. She is ninety-five, so I don't think she will get better this time.
4. My parents agreed to buy me a car. It's amazing news!
5. Yesterday my sister took my favorite shirt without asking. I'm still mad at her.

TRUE OR FALSE Track 024

Listen and write T for true or F for false.

1. **M** I often get nervous before I have an important exam. There are several things I do to make myself less nervous. Sometimes I go for a run. Other times I just lie down and listen to music. Studying right before the exam doesn't help. It just makes me more nervous, so I stop studying the day before the exam.
2. **W** My best friend Susan got married today. You should have seen her. She was beautiful in her long white gown. I've never seen her smile so much. I was worried that she would be nervous, but she wasn't at all. Overall it was a perfect day for her.
3. **W** You should see the new movie *War and Death*. It was so scary! I went by myself and actually screamed during the movie. I was holding onto the seat and had to close my eyes several times. It was great to feel that way, but next time I think I'll go see a comedy.

LISTENING PRACTICE Track 025

Listen and choose the correct answer.

Questions 1 and 2 refer to the following dialog.

M Are you angry at me? You seem upset.
W I'm not mad, I'm just disappointed.
M Why? What did I do?
W You were supposed to come to the movie theater yesterday afternoon. I waited for an hour, but you never showed up. I tried to call and text you, but you didn't answer your phone.

M Oh no! I'm so sorry. Please don't be annoyed. I forgot all about that. I dropped my phone, and I had to go with my mom to get it repaired. Then she wanted to get ice cream.

W I guess that's a good excuse. But I really wanted to see that movie.

Questions 3 and 4 refer to the following dialog.

W How's your job going these days, David?

M It's OK, I guess… Actually, it's not great.

W What's wrong?

M I'm sick and tired of working six days a week.

W You knew that the hours were long when you took the job.

M I know. But I didn't know how frustrated it would make me feel. Whenever my friends or family make plans for the weekend, I can't go.

W But you have Sundays off.

M I know, but my friends usually want to do stuff on Saturdays.

Questions 5 and 6 refer to the following talk.

M What do you do when you feel lonely? I usually call or text one of my friends. I'm sure you do the same thing. But what happens when they don't reply? Does it make you feel miserable? Do you worry that they are having fun without you? Does life make you feel confused? Do you worry about your future? If you answered yes to any of these questions, then you can benefit from my new book *Helping Yourself*. We can all change ourselves and have a positive attitude. And I can show you how!

DICTATION 1 Track 026

A. Listen and fill in the blanks.

1. We have to do a big homework assignment, but I didn't understand the instructions that the teacher gave us.
2. My boss wants me to stay late and finish a report, but I promised my wife that we would go to the movies.
3. My grandmother is sick again. She is ninety-five, so I don't think she will get better this time.
4. My parents agreed to buy me a car. It's amazing news!
5. Yesterday my sister took my favorite shirt without asking. I'm still mad at her.

B. Listen and fill in the blanks.

M Are you angry at me? You seem upset.

W I'm not mad, I'm just disappointed.

M Why? What did I do?

W You were supposed to come to the movie theater yesterday afternoon. I waited for an hour, but you never showed up. I tried to call and text you, but you didn't answer your phone.

M Oh no! I'm so sorry. Please don't be annoyed. I forgot all about that. I dropped my phone, and I had to go with my mom to get it repaired. Then she wanted to get ice cream.

W I guess that's a good excuse. But I really wanted to see that movie.

C. Listen and fill in the blanks.

W How's your job going these days, David?

M It's OK, I guess… Actually, it's not great.

W What's wrong?

M I'm sick and tired of working six days a week.

W You knew that the hours were long when you took the job.

M I know. But I didn't know how frustrated it would make me feel. Whenever my friends or family make plans for the weekend, I can't go.

W But you have Sundays off.

M I know, but my friends usually want to do stuff on Saturdays.

LISTENING TEST Track 027

Listen and choose the correct answer.

Questions 1 and 2 refer to the following dialog.

W I feel miserable.

M Why? What's wrong?

W Well, do you ever feel frustrated?

M Yes, especially when I study hard for a test but get a bad grade.

W Exactly. I worked really hard for my biology test, but when I looked at the questions, I couldn't remember anything.

M You probably did better than you think.

W No, I already got my result. I failed.

M Then you need to talk to your teacher. Maybe she can give you some advice on how to study more efficiently.

W I guess. I'm just embarrassed to talk to her when I got such a bad score.

M No, I'm sure she'll be happy to help you.

Questions 3 and 4 refer to the following dialog.

W Bill, you got 100% on this test.

M Did I really? I'm really surprised!
W Yes, I am very surprised as well. I have to ask you something, Bill. Did you copy your answers from Sam's test? You were sitting next to him, and your answers are almost the same as his.
M Um, well, yes. I'm afraid I did, Miss Parker. I didn't have time to study for the test.
W Oh, Bill! You're smart enough to pass this test without cheating.
M I'm sorry, Miss Parker. I've never cheated before, and I feel very bad.

Questions 5 and 6 refer to the following dialog.

M When do you get nervous, Karen?
W Nervous? I suppose when I have to speak in front of a group of people.
M Me too. I have to give a presentation in class next week and I really don't want to.
W I'm glad I don't have to do that. But my teacher gave me some good advice last year. She said I should practice my presentation in front of a mirror.
M Talk to myself in front of a mirror? That sounds crazy!
W No, it really helps. Practice talking, and time how long it takes. It will make you feel less nervous, and it will help you make sure your presentation is the right length.
M Hmm, maybe I'll try that.

DICTATION 2 Track 028

A. Listen and fill in the blanks.

W I feel miserable.
M Why? What's wrong?
W Well, do you ever feel frustrated?
M Yes, especially when I study hard for a test but get a bad grade.
W Exactly. I worked really hard for my biology test, but when I looked at the questions, I couldn't remember anything.
M You probably did better than you think.
W No, I already got my result. I failed.
M Then you need to talk to your teacher. Maybe she can give you some advice on how to study more efficiently.
W I guess. I'm just embarrassed to talk to her when I got such a bad score.
M No, I'm sure she'll be happy to help you.

B. Listen and fill in the blanks.

W Bill, you got 100% on this test.
M Did I really? I'm really surprised!
W Yes, I am very surprised as well. I have to ask you something, Bill. Did you copy your answers from Sam's test? You were sitting next to him, and your answers are almost the same as his.
M Um, well, yes. I'm afraid I did, Miss Parker. I didn't have time to study for the test.
W Oh, Bill! You're smart enough to pass this test without cheating.
M I'm sorry, Miss Parker. I've never cheated before, and I feel very bad.

C. Listen and fill in the blanks.

M When do you get nervous, Karen?
W Nervous? I suppose when I have to speak in front of a group of people.
M Me too. I have to give a presentation in class next week and I really don't want to.
W I'm glad I don't have to do that. But my teacher gave me some good advice last year. She said I should practice my presentation in front of a mirror.
M Talk to myself in front of a mirror? That sounds crazy!
W No, it really helps. Practice talking, and time how long it takes. It will make you feel less nervous, and it will help you make sure your presentation is the right length.
M Hmm, maybe I'll try that.

Unit 4 I Love It!

KEY WORDS Track 029

Listen for these words and phrases.

can't stand	love
used to	feel like
hate	healthy
prefer	rude
interested in	wait in line

KEY EXPRESSIONS Track 030

Listen and match each question with its correct answer.

1. Do you like reading?
2. How did you like that book I lent you?
3. What is something that annoys you?
4. What do you like to do on the weekend?
5. Do you have any hobbies?

WARM-UP Track 031

Listen and check what the speaker dislikes.

1. I can't stand people who are late for appointments. It's so rude to make someone wait.
2. My brother plays a lot of rock music. It's so loud, and it gives me a terrible headache.
3. My friends always want me to go out with them on Saturdays, but I don't enjoy going out.
4. My mom always makes me eat healthy foods, like broccoli and brown rice, but I'd prefer to eat pizza.
5. I used to like going out to nice restaurants, but now I prefer trying to cook new foods at home.

LISTEN FOR IT Track 032

Listen and check what the speaker likes.

1. The best way to spend a rainy day is to sit on the sofa and read a great book.
2. A lot of my friends hate math, but I love to study math. It's more interesting than reading.
3. It makes me very happy when I help other people. Because of this, I'm thinking about becoming a nurse.
4. My favorite place to go is the beach. I can swim in the sea, which is much better than a pool.
5. I always get up early because it makes me feel full of energy. I love watching the sun rise.

TRUE OR FALSE Track 033

Listen and write T for true or F for false.

1. **M** I'm crazy about music. My favorite is rock, but I also like jazz and pop. I even sometimes listen to classical music when I want to relax. The only music I really can't stand is rap. I just don't find it interesting. The only time that I don't listen to music is when I'm asleep.
2. **W** My husband and I watch a lot of TV. We both enjoy dramas and news programs, but that's where the similarities end. He likes to watch sports and reality TV shows, while I prefer comedies and mysteries. I love watching cooking shows the most, but my husband refuses to watch them.
3. **M** I'm very interested in China. I love to eat Chinese food, but don't really know how to cook it. I watch a lot of Chinese movies even though I don't understand the dialog. I just like the action. I hope to study Chinese in the future. My dream is to travel to China someday and be able to speak Chinese well.

LISTENING PRACTICE Track 034

Listen and choose the correct answer.

Questions 1 and 2 refer to the following dialog.

M Mary, do you like reading?
W Oh yes, I love to read.
M Do you read a lot of novels?
W Not really. I only read nonfiction because I prefer to learn something new while I am reading. And to be honest, I read more magazines than books.
M Which magazines do you like?
W I'm crazy about fashion magazines and nature magazines. I love to read about interesting animals. How about you? Do you read a lot?
M I don't read magazines, but I do like to read detective stories.

Questions 3 and 4 refer to the following talk.

W What is something that annoys you? I can't stand rude people. For example, I hate people who try to push in front when I am waiting in line. Please wait! I also hate people who use their phone when they are waiting at a traffic light. The light goes green, and their car doesn't move. They are too busy looking at their phone and they don't see the light change. It's rude behavior! Stop looking at your phone, everyone! Oh, and don't use your phone when you are at the movie theater. It's annoying to see the light from your phone when I am trying to watch the movie.

Questions 5 and 6 refer to the following dialog.

W What do you like to do on the weekend?
M It depends. I tend to stay at home, but sometimes I go out to a nice restaurant.
W I used to like going to restaurants, but I got bored of doing the same thing every week. And these days I'm trying to eat only healthy food.
M But there are so many different restaurants, and you can try something different every time. And you can order healthy food at a restaurant.
W I just don't enjoy it.
M I'm surprised. I love having the choice of different dishes to try.

DICTATION 1 Track 035

A. Listen and fill in the blanks.

1. The best way to spend a rainy day is to sit on the sofa and read a great book.
2. A lot of my friends hate math, but I love to study math. It's more interesting than reading.
3. It makes me very happy when I help other people. Because of this, I'm thinking about becoming a nurse.
4. My favorite place to go is the beach. I can swim in the sea, which is much better than a pool.
5. I always get up early because it makes me feel full of energy. I love watching the sun rise.

B. Listen and fill in the blanks.

M Mary, do you like reading?
W Oh yes, I love to read.
M Do you read a lot of novels?
W Not really. I only read nonfiction because I prefer to learn something new while I am reading. And to be honest, I read more magazines than books.
M Which magazines do you like?
W I'm crazy about fashion magazines and nature magazines. I love to read about interesting animals. How about you? Do you read a lot?
M I don't read magazines, but I do like to read detective stories.

C. Listen and fill in the blanks.

What is something that annoys you? I can't stand rude people. For example, I hate people who try to push in front when I am waiting in line. Please wait! I also hate people who use their phone when they are waiting at a traffic light. The light goes green, and their car doesn't move. They are too busy looking at their phone and they don't see the light change. It's rude behavior! Stop looking at your phone, everyone! Oh, and don't use your phone when you are at the movie theater. It's annoying to see the light from your phone when I am trying to watch the movie.

LISTENING TEST Track 036

Listen and choose the correct answer.

Questions 1 and 2 refer to the following dialog.

M How did you like that book I lent you?
W It was awful. I don't know why you gave it to me.
M You think so? I thought it was wonderful. What didn't you like about it?
W Well, for one thing, it was so long. I prefer reading short stories. And I didn't like the main character, Ruby. She was very rude and unfriendly. I wasn't interested in finding out what happened to her.
M I'm sorry that you didn't like it. I was going to recommend another book, but maybe that's not a good idea.
W I usually like the books you suggest, so go ahead.

Questions 3 and 4 refer to the following dialog.

W Do you have any hobbies?
M I'm into photography these days.
W That sounds like an expensive hobby.
M Not really. I mean, the camera was a little expensive, but I didn't buy a fancy one. You don't need to buy the best camera to take good photos.
W Do you print out your photos?
M No, I look at them on my computer, or I share them with my friends online. I think it's a waste of paper to print out lots of pictures.
W Yeah. And that would be expensive as well.

Questions 5 and 6 refer to the following dialog.

M Would you like to do something tonight?
W I don't feel like going out. Can we just hang out at home?
M Sure. Let's watch a movie.
W A movie sounds good. I downloaded a couple of movies the other day. Why don't we watch one of those?
M As long as they're not too serious. I'd like to watch something fun.
W Not a problem. They are both comedies. I heard that they are both really funny, so I think you'll like them both.
M Great. Let's watch them both.

DICTATION 2 Track 037

A. Listen and fill in the blanks.

M How did you like that book I lent you?
W It was awful. I don't know why you gave it to me.
M You think so? I thought it was wonderful. What didn't you like about it?
W Well, for one thing, it was so long. I prefer reading short stories. And I didn't like the main character, Ruby. She was very rude and unfriendly. I wasn't interested in finding out

what happened to her.

M I'm sorry that you didn't like it. I was going to recommend another book, but maybe that's not a good idea.

W I usually like the books you suggest, so go ahead.

B. Listen and fill in the blanks.

W Do you have any hobbies?

M I'm into photography these days.

W That sounds like an expensive hobby.

M Not really. I mean, the camera was a little expensive, but I didn't buy a fancy one. You don't need to buy the best camera to take good photos.

W Do you print out your photos?

M No, I look at them on my computer, or I share them with my friends online. I think it's a waste of paper to print out lots of pictures.

W Yeah. And that would be expensive as well.

C. Listen and fill in the blanks.

M Would you like to do something tonight?

W I don't feel like going out. Can we just hang out at home?

M Sure. Let's watch a movie.

W A movie sounds good. I downloaded a couple of movies the other day. Why don't we watch one of those?

M As long as they're not too serious. I'd like to watch something fun.

W Not a problem. They are both comedies. I heard that they are both really funny, so I think you'll like them both.

M Great. Let's watch them both.

Unit 5 Working Life

KEY WORDS Track 038

Listen for these words and phrases.

business person	doctor
architect	plumber
pension	dentist
employer	promotion
benefit	gardener

KEY EXPRESSIONS Track 039

Listen and match each question with its correct answer.

1. Is your job stressful?
2. How long have you been a teacher?
3. What do you do exactly?
4. Who do you work for?
5. How much vacation time do you get?

WARM-UP Track 040

Listen and check how the speaker feels about his or her job.

1. I work in sales, which I love. I'm very lucky to have a great employer.
2. I hoped to get a promotion this year, but I didn't. I've been here for six years, but I'm still in the same position.
3. My boss is going to send me to our Hong Kong branch for a year! It's amazing news!
4. I made a mistake in my business presentation, and now my boss wants to see me. I hope he won't fire me.
5. I have to work overtime almost every day. I'm just exhausted. I'm fed up with this job.

LISTEN FOR IT Track 041

Listen and check what kind of job would be good for the speaker.

1. I love reading, so it would be great to be around books all day.
2. I've always been good at growing flowers and plants. I also enjoy being outdoors.
3. My best subjects in school are math and science, especially biology. I also like helping people, so I want to work in a hospital.
4. I don't want to work in an office or sell things. I think I'd be good at fixing things.
5. My dream is to design school buildings. Most schools are ugly, so I want to make beautiful schools where everyone wants to study.

TRUE OR FALSE Track 042

Listen and write T for true or F for false.

1. **W** I'm not very happy with my current position. I work at Mel's Diner, where I'm a waitress. The hours are good, and it only takes me ten minutes to get to work by bus. It's my boss. He often criticizes me and says I'm slow. I do my best and customers like me, so I hope things improve soon.

2. **M** I have a great job. I teach at a small elementary school near my home. The kids are good, and the people I work with are nice. The salary isn't so great, but I get good benefits like a pension and lots of vacation. It's wonderful to get every summer off.
3. **W** My father has done many things. He was originally going to be an architect but decided to study accounting instead. After working as an accountant for a while, he quit and became a writer. Then he got a job as a reporter for our city newspaper. I wouldn't be surprised if he switches jobs again someday.

LISTENING PRACTICE Track 043

Listen and choose the correct answer.

Questions 1 and 2 refer to the following dialog.

M Who do you work for?
W I work for ABC Technology. I've been there for about four years.
M What do you do exactly?
W I sell new products to stores in three different cities. We develop computer accessories, so it's my job to persuade stores to stock our products.
M Do you enjoy it?
W Yes, I get to meet a lot of people, and I have to visit a lot of stores every day, so I don't spend the day sitting at a desk. It's fun to explain our new products to other people.
M That sounds like an interesting job.

Questions 3 and 4 refer to the following talk.

W My father recently got a promotion at work. He works really hard, so we are all proud of him. He moved from assistant manager to executive manager at the architect's office where he works. He got a pay increase of 5%, and he is now in charge of more people. He also gets a company car now. He used to supervise 15 people, but now he is in charge of 30 people. He has a lot more work to do. He seems to work longer hours now, and I think he has a bit more stress, but I'm sure he will get used to it.

Questions 5 and 6 refer to the following dialog.

W What do you do for a living?
M I'm a teacher.
W No kidding? How long have you been a teacher?
M I've been teaching since 2015. I always wanted to be a teacher, even when I was in elementary school.
W What grade do you teach?
M First grade. The students are so cute and they all want to learn. It's a great feeling to teach new skills to such young children.
W Do you want to try teaching other grades as well?
M Maybe second grade, but I don't really want to teach older students. I'm better with the youngest students.

DICTATION 1 Track 044

A. Listen and fill in the blanks.

1. I love reading, so it would be great to be around books all day.
2. I've always been good at growing flowers and plants. I also enjoy being outdoors.
3. My best subjects in school are math and science, especially biology. I also like helping people, so I want to work in a hospital.
4. I don't want to work in an office or sell things. I think I'd be good at fixing things.
5. My dream is to design school buildings. Most schools are ugly, so I want to make beautiful schools where everyone wants to study.

B. Listen and fill in the blanks.

M Who do you work for?
W I work for ABC Technology. I've been there for about four years.
M What do you do exactly?
W I sell new products to stores in three different cities. We develop computer accessories, so it's my job to persuade stores to stock our products.
M Do you enjoy it?
W Yes, I get to meet a lot of people, and I have to visit a lot of stores every day, so I don't spend the day sitting at a desk. It's fun to explain our new products to other people.
M That sounds like an interesting job.

C. Listen and fill in the blanks.

My father recently got a promotion at work. He works really hard so we are all proud of him. He moved from assistant manager to executive manager at the architect's office where he works. He got a pay increase of 5% and he is now in charge of more people. He also gets a company car now. He used to supervise 15 people, but now he is in charge of 30 people. He has a lot more work to do. He seems to work longer hours now and I think he has a bit more stress, but I'm sure he will get used to it.

LISTENING TEST Track 045

Listen and choose the correct answer.

Questions 1 and 2 refer to the following dialog.

W OK, Mr. Smith. Well, you seem to be generally healthy, but your heart is a little fast. Is your job stressful?

M Only when I have a big project to complete. I'm a plumber, and most of my jobs are small. But I work for myself, not an employer, so it's sometimes difficult to take a break or a vacation.

W How many hours do you work without a break?

M Most days I work from 8:00 a.m. until 6:00 p.m., but if the job is difficult, I might have to work until as late as ten o'clock at night.

W I see. Well, I think you need to start taking some more breaks, for your health.

Questions 3 and 4 refer to the following dialog.

M How long have you been with your company, Daniella?

W For about six months.

M How do you like it so far?

W It's going well. I'm really glad that I studied business studies. It is really helping me to be a good business person.

M How much vacation time do you get?

W I get ten paid days off a year, but that will increase to twelve after two years, and fifteen days after three.

M Do you get any benefits?

W There is a company pension, and I can get a discount on a gym membership. And there is free breakfast in the staff break room.

Questions 5 and 6 refer to the following dialog.

M Long time no see, Liz.

W Felix! It's great to see you. I heard that you opened a gardening business.

M That's right. I love gardening, so I thought I might as well get paid to do it. So now I have my own company. There are three of us working as gardeners.

W Nice. I work for Johnson Dental Clinic—the one on 3rd Street.

M Oh really? Are you a dental assistant?

W Actually, I'm a dentist.

M Oh, well done! That's great. You always were the smart one in the class!

DICTATION 2 Track 046

A. Listen and fill in the blanks.

W OK, Mr. Smith. Well, you seem to be generally healthy, but your heart is a little fast. Is your job stressful?

M Only when I have a big project to complete. I'm a plumber, and most of my jobs are small. But I work for myself, not an employer, so it's sometimes difficult to take a break or a vacation.

W How many hours do you work without a break?

M Most days I work from 8:00 a.m. until 6:00 p.m., but if the job is difficult, I might have to work until as late as ten o'clock at night.

W I see. Well, I think you need to start taking some more breaks, for your health.

B. Listen and fill in the blanks.

M How long have you been with your company, Daniella?

W For about six months.

M How do you like it so far?

W It's going well. I'm really glad that I studied business studies. It is really helping me to be a good business person.

M How much vacation time do you get?

W I get ten paid days off a year, but that will increase to twelve after two years, and fifteen days after three.

M Do you get any benefits?

W There is a company pension, and I can get a discount on a gym membership. And there is free breakfast in the staff break room.

C. Listen and fill in the blanks.

M Long time no see, Liz.

W Felix! It's great to see you. I heard that you opened a gardening business.

M That's right. I love gardening, so I thought I might as well get paid to do it. So now I have my own company. There are three of us working as gardeners.

W Nice. I work for Johnson Dental Clinic—the one on 3rd Street.

M Oh really? Are you a dental assistant?
W Actually, I'm a dentist.
M Oh, well done! That's great. You always were the smart one in the class!

Unit 6 School Life

KEY WORDS Track 047

Listen for these words and phrases.

medical school
literature
university
social studies
graduate school
law
cram (for an exam)
bachelor's degree
chemistry
tuition fees

KEY EXPRESSIONS Track 048

Listen and match each question with its correct answer.

1. What year are you in?
2. How many classes are you taking this semester?
3. What grade did you get on the last test?
4. What do you want to do after you graduate?
5. Did you get into medical school?

WARM-UP Track 049

Listen and check what the speaker plans to study.

1. I love to read, and I think I'd like to be a writer, so I'm going to study American literature.
2. I want to be a doctor. It's my dream job, so after I graduate, I'm going to medical school.
3. I'm very interested in science, and I want to invent a new drug when I'm older, so I plan to study chemistry at university.
4. I want to learn more about different cultures and societies, so I will study social studies.
5. I want to help people, but I also like to think deeply about difficult issues. I think it would be exciting to go to court and speak in front of a judge.

LISTEN FOR IT Track 050

Listen and check the subject the speaker liked best in school.

1. I wasn't good at P.E. or science, but I really enjoyed social studies when I was a student.
2. The only class I was good at in school was math, but English was my favorite.
3. I liked chemistry the most in high school because I liked doing experiments.
4. I was never a very good student, but I did enjoy history. I had a great teacher.
5. I used to like classes where I could make something. That's why I enjoyed art so much.

TRUE OR FALSE Track 051

Listen and write T for true or F for false.

1. **M** I wasn't very happy with my grades this semester. My favorite class was history, but I only managed to get a B. I got an A in English which surprised me. But I got a C in math and I got a D in social studies. It's the first D I've ever received.
2. **W** My brother Robin is a senior in college. He's about to graduate with a bachelor's degree in engineering. My mother wants him to go to graduate school, but Robin wants to get a job. He says the tuition fees for graduate school are too high.
3. **M** College is very different from high school. I have fewer classes every week, but I have a lot more homework and assignments to do. I go to the library for three hours after my last class. It's easier for me to study there than at home.

LISTENING PRACTICE Track 052

Listen and choose the correct answer.

Questions 1 and 2 refer to the following dialog.

W What year are you in?
M I'm a senior.
W In college?
M No, I'm still in high school, but I'm going to college next year.
W Do you know what you will study in college?
M I hope to go to medical school eventually, so I plan to get a bachelor's degree in chemistry first. I'll also take a lot of math and biology classes, of course.
W It sounds like you have planned out your future well.
M I hope so, but I know that I have a lot of work to do if I want to succeed.
W Well, good luck, Simon.

Questions 3 and 4 refer to the following talk.

I have a big exam tomorrow. It's for my social studies class. I find the class a bit boring, so I didn't really study much. Now I have to cram for the exam tonight. My teachers all say that it's bad to cram for an exam. I think they are probably right because I forget everything that I learned right after the exam. Maybe I would remember more if I studied more carefully over several weeks. Anyway, it's too late now! Wish me luck, because I'm going to need it! It's OK if I get a C. I just don't want to fail.

Questions 5 and 6 refer to the following dialog.

M How do you like university life so far?
W I like it a lot. My major is English literature, and I have some interesting professors.
M Are you living with your parents?
W No, I'm renting a room near the university.
M What do you want to do after you graduate?
W I think I'll probably go to graduate school. Actually, I don't know yet. I might apply for law school right after I get my degree. Or maybe I'll work for a couple of years first.
M You have a few years before you have to decide, so no need to hurry into a decision.

DICTATION 1 Track 053

A. Listen and fill in the blanks.

1. I wasn't good at P.E. or science, but I really enjoyed social studies when I was a student.
2. The only class I was good at in school was math, but English was my favorite.
3. I liked chemistry the most in high school because I liked doing experiments.
4. I was never a very good student, but I did enjoy history. I had a great teacher.
5. I used to like classes where I could make something. That's why I enjoyed art so much.

B. Listen and fill in the blanks.

W What year are you in?
M I'm a senior.
W In college?
M No, I'm still in high school, but I'm going to college next year.
W Do you know what you will study in college?
M I hope to go to medical school eventually, so I plan to get a bachelor's degree in chemistry first. I'll also take a lot of math and biology classes, of course.
W It sounds like you have planned out your future well.
M I hope so, but I know that I have a lot of work to do if I want to succeed.
W Well, good luck, Simon.

C. Listen and fill in the blanks.

I have a big exam tomorrow. It's for my social studies class. I find the class a bit boring, so I didn't really study much. Now I have to cram for the exam tonight. My teachers all say that it's bad to cram for an exam. I think they are probably right because I forget everything that I learned right after the exam. Maybe I would remember more if I studied more carefully over several weeks. Anyway, it's too late now! Wish me luck, because I'm going to need it! It's OK if I get a C. I just don't want to fail.

LISTENING TEST Track 054

Listen and choose the correct answer.

Questions 1 and 2 refer to the following dialog.

W How many classes are you taking?
M I'm taking three this time. I was going to take French but decided against it.
W Are you taking chemistry? I was hoping we could be study partners.
M Yes, I'm taking chemistry, history, and a math class.
W OK, I'm taking chemistry and French. Have you taken French?
M No, but I took Korean last year. It was really cool to learn a new way of writing.
W That sounds really difficult. French is hard enough for me, and that uses the same alphabet as English!

Questions 3 and 4 refer to the following dialog.

M Hey, Miranda! Did you get into medical school?
W Yes, I start in the fall.
M Wow, that's great. You must be so excited.
W Yeah, but now I'm worrying about the tuition fees.
M But you knew it was expensive when you applied.
W Yes, I did, but I didn't really think that I would be accepted. So now I have to borrow a lot of money to pay for my tuition.
M But that's normal for medical students. All your classmates will have to do the same. It's fine. You'll make lots of money after you graduate.

Questions 5 and 6 refer to the following dialog.

M Have you finished the math homework, Sonya?
W Not quite, but I'm almost done.
M Can you help me with a couple of the problems? I don't understand how to do them.
W Sure. Hey, what grade did you get on the last test?
M I got a B, but I really wanted an A.
W I can help you study for the next test if you like. I'm doing really well in this class.
M That would be great.
W Let's get something to eat, then go to the library for a while?
M Sure. It's hard to study when I'm hungry!

DICTATION 2 Track 055

A. Listen and fill in the blanks.

W How many classes are you taking?
M I'm taking three this time. I was going to take French but decided against it.
W Are you taking chemistry? I was hoping we could be study partners.
M Yes, I'm taking chemistry, history, and a math class.
W OK, I'm taking chemistry and French. Have you taken French?
M No, but I took Korean last year. It was really cool to learn a new way of writing.
W That sounds really difficult. French is hard enough for me, and that uses the same alphabet as English!

B. Listen and fill in the blanks.

M Hey Miranda! Did you get into medical school?
W Yes, I start in the fall.
M Wow, that's great. You must be so excited.
W Yeah, but now I'm worrying about the tuition fees.
M But you knew it was expensive when you applied.
W Yes, I did, but I didn't really think that I would be accepted. So now I have to borrow a lot of money to pay for my tuition.
M But that's normal for medical students. All your classmates will have to do the same. It's fine. You'll make lots of money after you graduate.

C. Listen and fill in the blanks.

M Have you finished the math homework, Sonya?
W Not quite, but I'm almost done.
M Can you help me with a couple of the problems? I don't understand how to do them.
W Sure. Hey, what grade did you get on the last test?
M I got a B, but I really wanted an A.
W I can help you study for the next test if you like. I'm doing really well in this class.
M That would be great.
W Let's get something to eat, then go to the library for a while?
M Sure. It's hard to study when I'm hungry!

Unit 7 A New Home

KEY WORDS Track 056

Listen for these words and phrases.

realtor	townhouse
upstairs	studio apartment
view	redecorate
air conditioner	recently
furniture	condominium

KEY EXPRESSIONS Track 057

Listen and match each question with its correct answer.

1. Do you mind if I turn down the air conditioner?
2. Do you live in the city?
3. How long have you lived here?
4. Have you finished redecorating your new place?
5. Have you met your neighbors?

WARM-UP Track 058

Listen and check where the speaker lives.

1. I just bought a townhouse. It has three floors and a small garden.
2. I was tired of living and working in the crowded city, so I bought a farm!
3. It was too much work to take care of my garden, so I moved to a condominium.
4. I was going to buy a townhouse, but I decided it was too big, so I bought a studio apartment instead.
5. I don't like driving a long way to work, so I moved to a place downtown.

LISTEN FOR IT Track 059

Listen and check which room the speaker is talking about.

1. Do you like the new sink and counter? It's so much more fun to cook now!
2. I bought new furniture to celebrate my new job. My new sofa and armchairs are very comfortable.
3. Thanks to my new bed, I finally sleep well at night.
4. My kids are lucky because they have a room where they can store and play with all their toys.
5. The shower and sink are both new. The window gives the room lots of light.

TRUE OR FALSE Track 060

Listen and write T for true or F for false.

1. **M** I recently moved into a condominium. Now I'm redecorating it. The walls were an ugly brown, but I'm painting everything blue. It's a two-bedroom place in the suburbs. It's a nice change from the city. I haven't met my neighbors yet. I'll probably invite them over for a small party after I get settled.
2. **W** And now we're moving into the kitchen. This kitchen is big enough for a large family. There's plenty of counter space, as you can see. Over there is a good place for a microwave, if you have one. The refrigerator and stove are included in the home price. These cupboards are all new and have been recently painted.
3. **M** My wife Gail and I have recently purchased a beautiful home. It has a large garden and a yard for the kids. Inside, there's a kitchen, living room, dining room and bathroom. Upstairs, there's our bedroom plus separate bedrooms for our two kids. There's plenty of room, and we're happy to be first-time home-owners.

LISTENING PRACTICE Track 061

Listen and choose the correct answer.

Questions 1 and 2 refer to the following dialog.

W Have you finished redecorating your bedroom?
M Almost, but there are still a few things to do. The store already delivered the bed and drawers. But we still need to paint the walls.
W What color are you painting them?
M Actually, it's hard to decide. I think blue would be good, but my wife wants to paint them green.
W Why don't you paint three walls one color, and paint the last wall the other color? It's popular these days.
M That's an interesting idea.
W Plus, blue and green look good together. It'll look nice.

Questions 3 and 4 refer to the following dialog.

W So this is a townhouse?
M Yes, I love it because I have a great view from the top floor.
W But you have to go upstairs and down again several times a day.
M It's fine for me.
W There are too many stairs for me. It seems very tiring. Have you met your neighbors?
M Yes, we went and introduced ourselves when we first moved in. They seem nice.
W You should invite them to dinner.
M We probably will.

Questions 5 and 6 refer to the following dialog.

W Thank you for coming.
M You have a very nice house. How long have you lived here?
W We've been in this house for about three years. Hey, it's a little warm in here. Would you mind if I turn on the air conditioner?
M Of course not. Go ahead. I'm a little hot myself.
W Can I get you something to drink? I made some iced tea earlier.
M That sounds good. By the way, who was your realtor? I'm thinking of moving out of my condominium, but I need some good advice.
W Her name was Sheila Kim. I'll send you her details.

DICTATION 1 Track 062

A. Listen and fill in the blanks.

1. Do you like the new sink and counter? It's so much more fun to cook now!
2. I bought new furniture to celebrate my new job. My new sofa and armchairs are very comfortable.
3. Thanks to my new bed, I finally sleep well at night.
4. My kids are lucky because they have a room where they can store and play with all their toys.
5. The shower and sink are both new. The window gives the room lots of light.

B. Listen and fill in the blanks.

W Have you finished redecorating your bedroom?
M Almost, but there are still a few things to do. The store already delivered the bed and drawers. But we still need to paint the walls.

W What color are you painting them?
M Actually, it's hard to decide. I think blue would be good, but my wife wants to paint them green.
W Why don't you paint three walls one color, and paint the last wall the other color? It's popular these days.
M That's an interesting idea.
W Plus, blue and green look good together. It'll look nice.

C. Listen and fill in the blanks.

W So this is a townhouse?
M Yes, I love it because I have a great view from the top floor.
W But you have to go upstairs and down again several times a day.
M It's fine for me.
W There are too many stairs for me. It seems very tiring. Have you met your neighbors?
M Yes, we went and introduced ourselves when we first moved in. They seem nice.
W You should invite them to dinner.
M We probably will.

LISTENING TEST Track 063

Listen and choose the correct answer.

Questions 1 and 2 refer to the following dialog.

W Do you live in the city, Tom?
M No, I recently moved to the suburbs.
W I sometimes think about moving to the suburbs. I have a studio apartment in the city center.
M I used to rent an apartment downtown, but I wanted more space. I have a dog, so an apartment wasn't good for him.
W So where do you live?
M I have a house on Freeport Road, near the library.
W That's a nice area. I sometimes go for walks in that neighborhood.
M Yes, it's very quiet, and there is a nice park with tennis courts near my house.

Questions 3 and 4 refer to the following dialog.

M What do you do for a living, Soo Kyung?
W I'm a realtor. I help people buy and sell houses.
M What do you like most about your job?
W I like looking inside other people's houses. It's very interesting. It gives me lots of ideas for decorating my own home.
M But I'm sure you see some ugly houses, too.
W I do, and I hate visiting houses that don't have air conditioning in the summer. But most of the time, I really enjoy my job.
M It sounds interesting.

Questions 5 and 6 refer to the following dialog.

M Come in. Dinner's almost ready.
W I'm sorry I'm late. I had some trouble finding your house.
M Yes, the streets can be a little confusing around here.
W How many rooms do you have?
M Four. The kitchen is through that door and my bedroom's over there.
W Where's the bathroom?
M In there. Why don't you have a seat?
W OK. Your sofa looks comfortable.

DICTATION 2 Track 064

A. Listen and fill in the blanks.

W Do you live in the city, Tom?
M No, I recently moved to the suburbs.
W I sometimes think about moving to the suburbs. I have a studio apartment in the city center.
M I used to rent an apartment downtown, but I wanted more space. I have a dog, so an apartment wasn't good for him.
W So where do you live?
M I have a house on Freeport Road, near the library.
W That's a nice area. I sometimes go for walks in that neighborhood.
M Yes, it's very quiet, and there is a nice park with tennis courts near my house.

B. Listen and fill in the blanks.

M What do you do for a living, Soo Kyung?
W I'm a realtor. I help people buy and sell houses.
M What do you like most about your job?
W I like looking inside other people's houses. It's very interesting. It gives me lots of ideas for decorating my own home.
M But I'm sure you see some ugly houses, too.
W I do, and I hate visiting houses that don't have air conditioning in the summer. But most of the time, I really enjoy my job.
M It sounds interesting.

C. Listen and fill in the blanks.

M Come in. Dinner's almost ready.
W I'm sorry I'm late. I had some trouble finding your house.

M Yes, the streets can be a little confusing around here.
W How many rooms do you have?
M Four. The kitchen is through that door and my bedroom's over there.
W Where's the bathroom?
M In there. Why don't you have a seat?
W OK. Your sofa looks comfortable.

Unit 8 Places to Go

KEY WORDS Track 065

Listen for these words and phrases.

reservation
cruise
aisle seat
carry-on
hotel lobby
passport
confirm
boarding pass
travel agent
beach resort

KEY EXPRESSIONS Track 066

Listen and match each question with its correct answer.

1. I'd like to confirm a flight, please.
2. Have you ever been abroad?
3. Would you like a window or an aisle seat?
4. May I see your passport, please?
5. What time should I check out?

WARM-UP Track 067

Listen and check where the speaker is going on vacation.

1. My family and I love to swim and spend time playing on the beach, so we are going to a resort in Hawaii this summer.
2. My wife is taking French lessons, so we are going to Paris this year.
3. My parents said we are going to go camping in the mountains this summer. But I wanted to go to Disneyland.
4. I'm going on a cruise for a whole month! I can't wait.
5. I like to travel and learn new things, so I'm going to a cooking school in Italy for one week.

LISTEN FOR IT Track 068

Listen and check where the speaker went for their last vacation.

1. I spent two weeks on a cruise ship last summer. I stopped in Spain, Portugal, Italy, and France.
2. I recently got a job in Thailand, so I spent my last vacation in Cambodia because it is near there.
3. I don't like traveling because I don't like hotels, so I stayed at home last year.
4. My holiday in New York and Boston was so much fun last winter, even though it was cold.
5. I went to visit my aunt who lives in China a couple of months ago. It was great.

TRUE OR FALSE Track 069

Listen and write T for true or F for false.

1. **M** I have your flight tickets ready. You leave New York June 3rd at 9:00 a.m. You fly to Dallas, where you arrive at 11:30. At 12:45, you transfer planes and arrive in Los Angeles at 2:30. If you want to change your flight schedule at all, please call me.
2. **W** I really enjoyed my vacation in Hong Kong. I was there for five days and four nights. My hotel was very basic, but I didn't spend much time in my room. I spent a lot of time shopping at the wonderful malls there. Of course, I also spent a lot of money.
3. **W** I'm flying to Dallas on business next week. I could take a train, but flying is only slightly more expensive than the train. And it saves time. The flight is direct, so it will take me about an hour to get there. The train would take almost three hours.

LISTENING PRACTICE Track 070

Listen and choose the correct answer.

Questions 1 and 2 refer to the following dialog.

W Hello. Giselle's Travel.
M I'd like to confirm a flight, please.
W Can I have your name and flight number?
M Yes, it's Jonathon Fielding, Flight 755.
W OK, you're confirmed, Mr. Fielding, on Flight 755 for this Friday morning. Please note that the departure time has changed.
M Oh, really?
W Yes, the flight now leaves London Heathrow at 8:30 instead of 8:00. You will arrive in Seoul thirty minutes later than originally scheduled.
M That's even better! I can sleep a little longer on Friday.

Questions 3 and 4 refer to the following dialog.

M Have you ever been abroad?
W Yes. I went to Europe last year.

M How was it? What cities did you visit?
W I flew to Paris, then I took a train to Milan and Rome. It was amazing.
M Didn't you visit London? I've always wanted to go there.
W No, I didn't have enough time, but I did go through Switzerland on the train. The view of the mountains was beautiful.
M I'd really like to visit another country some day. I need to save up enough money first.

Questions 5 and 6 refer to the following dialog.

W May I see your passport, please?
M Here you are.
W Thank you, Mr. Lee. Would you like a window or an aisle seat?
M Aisle, please.
W OK, and do you have any bags to check in?
M No, I only have this carry-on.
W Thank you. Here's your boarding pass. Your seat number is 22C, which is an aisle seat. Please go to passport control and be at Gate 20 by 11:15. The flight leaves at twelve. Have a great flight.
M Thank you.

DICTATION 1 Track 071

A. Listen and fill in the blanks.

1. I spent two weeks on a cruise ship last summer. I stopped in Spain, Portugal, Italy, and France.
2. I recently got a job in Thailand, so I spent my last vacation in Cambodia because it is near there.
3. I don't like traveling because I don't like hotels, so I stayed at home last year.
4. My holiday in New York and Boston was so much fun last winter, even though it was cold.
5. I went to visit my aunt who lives in China a couple of months ago. It was great.

B. Listen and fill in the blanks.

W Hello. Giselle's Travel.
M I'd like to confirm a flight, please.
W Can I have your name and flight number?
M Yes, it's Jonathon Fielding, Flight 755.
W OK, you're confirmed, Mr. Fielding, on Flight 755 for this Friday morning. Please note that the departure time has changed.
M Oh really?
W Yes, the flight now leaves London Heathrow at 8:30 instead of 8:00. You will arrive in Seoul thirty minutes later than originally scheduled.
M That's even better! I can sleep a little longer on Friday.

C. Listen and fill in the blanks.

M Have you ever been abroad?
W Yes. I went to Europe last year.
M How was it? What cities did you visit?
W I flew to Paris, then I took a train to Milan and Rome. It was amazing.
M Didn't you visit London? I've always wanted to go there.
W No, I didn't have enough time, but I did go through Switzerland on the train. The view of the mountains was beautiful.
M I'd really like to visit another country someday. I need to save up enough money first.

LISTENING TEST Track 072

Listen and choose the correct answer.

Questions 1 and 2 refer to the following dialog.

M Oh, look, Ji-Min! There's a sign for the beach resort. And here is the resort.
W It's smaller than I expected. It looked much bigger in the pictures that travel agent showed us.
M It looks fine to me. Why don't you wait here in the hotel lobby while I check in?
W No, I'll come with you. They'll probably need to see my passport, and I have a few questions.
M I hope you aren't going to complain about anything.
W No, of course not. I want to ask about breakfast. I can't remember if it is included in the price or not.
M I think it's included, but you can ask.

Questions 3 and 4 refer to the following dialog.

M Good evening, ma'am. May I see your boarding pass and passport?
W Here you are. I have my children's passports as well. For my son and my daughter.
M Thank you. Where are you traveling from?
W We flew in from Chicago. We're going on a cruise.
M I see. How long will you be here in London?
W Just one night. Our cruise leaves tomorrow.
M And can you give me the address of the hotel where you are staying tonight?
W Yes. It's Hotel Windsor, Chancery Lane.

Questions 5 and 6 refer to the following dialog.

W Hello, I have a reservation under the name Samantha Baker.

M Ah, yes, Miss Baker. You are staying with us for three nights.

W That's right.

M I see you booked a non-smoking room with an ocean view. A single room. That all looks good. You are in room 712, which is on the 7th floor.

W Great. What time should I check out?

M Check out is at 11 a.m.

DICTATION 2 Track 073

A. Listen and fill in the blanks.

M Oh, look Ji-Min! There's a sign for the beach resort. And here is the resort.

W It's smaller than I expected. It looked much bigger in the pictures that travel agent showed us.

M It looks fine to me. Why don't you wait here in the hotel lobby while I check in?

W No, I'll come with you. They'll probably need to see my passport, and I have a few questions.

M I hope you aren't going to complain about anything.

W No, of course not. I want to ask about breakfast. I can't remember if it is included in the price or not.

M I think it's included, but you can ask.

B. Listen and fill in the blanks.

M Good evening, ma'am. May I see your boarding pass and passport?

W Here you are. I have my children's passports as well. For my son and my daughter.

M Thank you. Where are you traveling from?

W We flew in from Chicago. We're going on a cruise.

M I see. How long will you be here in London?

W Just one night. Our cruise leaves tomorrow.

M And can you give me the address of the hotel where you are staying tonight?

W Yes. It's Hotel Windsor, Chancery Lane.

C. Listen and fill in the blanks.

W Hello, I have a reservation under the name Samantha Baker.

M Ah, yes, Miss Baker. You are staying with us for three nights.

W That's right.

M I see you booked a non-smoking room with an ocean view. A single room. That all looks good. You are in room 712, which is on the 7th floor.

W Great. What time should I check out?

M Checkout is at 11 a.m.

Unit 9 Plans and Appointments

KEY WORDS Track 074

Listen for these words and phrases.

appointment	cancel
available	free
urgent	suit
run late	arrange
picnic	date

KEY EXPRESSIONS Track 075

Listen and match each question with its correct answer.

1. Are you free this evening?
2. Are you coming to the picnic tomorrow?
3. What time should I come?
4. Have you arranged food for the party?
5. How about going to a baseball game next week?

WARM-UP Track 076

Listen and check what the speaker has to do today.

1. It's my friend's birthday today, so I have to buy her a gift.
2. I have a toothache, so I need to make an appointment with the dentist.
3. I'm so nervous. I have to make a presentation in my English class today.
4. I have to bake a cake for my parents' wedding anniversary. I hope I don't burn it!
5. I don't have to do anything today! It's a holiday, and I don't have any plans.

LISTEN FOR IT Track 077

Listen and check why the speaker had to cancel their plans.

1. I was going to play computer games at my friend's house, but my mom says I have to visit my grandmother.
2. I arranged a soccer game with my friends, but it is pouring rain, so we can't play.
3. I planned to go to a movie with my sister, but I have a terrible headache.

4. I arranged to take today off, but my boss wants me to finish an urgent report instead.
5. I lost my wallet, so I can't pay for my train ticket to the beach. I'll have to stay at home.

TRUE OR FALSE Track 078

Listen and write T for true or F for false.

1. **M** Sherry, I just wanted to let you know that I'm running late. I have to talk to my boss, but I'll get to the restaurant as soon as I can. I should be there by 6:30. I'll call you when I leave work.
2. **M** I don't feel like doing anything tonight. I worked all day and am really exhausted. I want to stay home and maybe watch some TV, but I promised Barbara I would meet her for dinner. I should call her and tell her I don't want to go, but I promised her I would be there. I know she will be disappointed if I don't go.
3. **M** Mr. Livingston, I'd like to go over your schedule for tomorrow. You have a meeting with a client at 10:00, and at 12:00 you'll be having lunch with Alex Robbins. Your sales presentation has been postponed until Friday. From 2:00 to 3:00, you'll be discussing next year's budget with Mr. Jones.

LISTENING PRACTICE Track 079

Listen and choose the correct answer.

Questions 1 and 2 refer to the following dialog.

W Hi, Mike. What's up? I'm calling to see if you want to watch a movie or something.
M Hi, Susan. I'm just getting ready to go out.
W Do you have a date tonight?
M Yes. I'm going to a concert with Blake. Remember? We're going to see Allie Felix at the Downtown Arena.
W Oh, right. That's tonight? Well, I'd better let you finish getting ready.
M Yeah, I'm running a little late.
W OK. Give me a call tomorrow and we can make plans for next week. I hope you have a good time tonight.

Questions 3 and 4 refer to the following talk.

M I wish it were the summer vacation already. But I have school for two more weeks. I have a math exam on Tuesday, an English exam on Wednesday, and a chemistry exam the week after. But I can't study much this weekend because it's my mom's birthday and she wants the whole family to go on a big picnic. It will be fun, but I really need to study. I think I will do well in my English exam, but I'm not very good at math and chemistry.

Questions 5 and 6 refer to the following dialog.

M Hello, Dr. Morton's office.
W Hi, I'm afraid I need to cancel my appointment. Something urgent came up at work, and I can't go.
M Thank you for calling to let us know. What's the name?
W Hall. Tracey Hall. It's a 3 o'clock appointment.
M OK, Tracey. Would you like to make a new appointment?
W Um, do you have any appointments for tomorrow afternoon?
M Yes, Dr. Morton is available at 2:30 tomorrow. Would that suit you?
W Yes, thank you.

DICTATION 1 Track 080

A. Listen and fill in the blanks.

1. **M** I was going to play computer games at my friend's house, but my mom says I have to visit my grandmother.
2. **W** I arranged a soccer game with my friends, but it is pouring rain, so we can't play.
3. **M** I planned to go to a movie with my sister, but I have a terrible headache.
4. **W** I arranged to take today off, but my boss wants me to finish an urgent report instead.
5. **M** I lost my wallet, so I can't pay for my train ticket to the beach. I'll have to stay at home.

B. Listen and fill in the blanks.

W Hi, Mike. What's up? I'm calling to see if you want to watch a movie or something.
M Hi, Susan. I'm just getting ready to go out.
W Do you have a date tonight?
M Yes. I'm going to a concert with Blake. Remember? We're going to see Allie Felix at the Downtown Arena.
W Oh, right. That's tonight? Well, I'd better let you finish getting ready.
M Yeah, I'm running a little late.
W OK. Give me a call tomorrow, and we can make plans for next week. I hope you have a good time tonight.

C. Listen and fill in the blanks.

I wish it were the summer vacation already. But I have school for two more weeks. I have a math exam on Tuesday, an English exam on Wednesday, and a chemistry exam the week after. But I can't study much this weekend because it's my mom's birthday and she wants the whole family to go on a big picnic. It will be fun, but I really need to study. I think I will do well on my English exam, but I'm not very good at math and chemistry.

LISTENING TEST Track 081

Listen and choose the correct answer.

Questions 1 and 2 refer to the following dialog.

W Are you coming to the picnic tomorrow?
M I'll try to go. But I'm not sure yet if I can make it.
W Why's that?
M I have church until 11:00.
W That's not a problem. It doesn't really start until noon.
M In that case, I think I can go.
W Come anytime. It'll go until 5:00.
M Should I bring something to eat or drink?
W No, just bring yourself!

Questions 3 and 4 refer to the following dialog.

W Hi, Joe. I'm excited about your party tomorrow. What time should I come?
M Come to my apartment any time after 6:00.
W Sounds good. Have you arranged food for the party?
M Yes, my mom and her friends are going to cook.
W That's nice of them. Is your mom coming to the party?
M No, she said she'd bring the food, then she's going to a movie with her friends.
W I hope you are paying for their tickets.
M Hey, that's a good idea. What a great thank-you gift!

Questions 5 and 6 refer to the following dialog.

M Are you free this evening?
W No, I have to study for a math exam tonight.
M That's too bad. Well, do you need any help studying? You know that I'm really good at math.
W No, that's OK. I study better alone.
M How about going to a baseball game next week?
W That sounds like fun. I'll have plenty of time next week.
M Great. I'll check the days and times of the games.

DICTATION 2 Track 082

A. Listen and fill in the blanks.

W Are you coming to the picnic tomorrow?
M I'll try to go. But I'm not sure yet if I can make it.
W Why's that?
M I have church until 11:00.
W That's not a problem. It doesn't really start until noon.
M In that case, I think I can go.
W Come anytime. It'll go until 5:00.
M Should I bring something to eat or drink?
W No, just bring yourself!

B. Listen and fill in the blanks.

W Hi, Joe. I'm excited about your party tomorrow. What time should I come?
M Come to my apartment any time after 6:00.
W Sounds good. Have you arranged food for the party?
M Yes, my mom and her friends are going to cook.
W That's nice of them. Is your mom coming to the party?
M No, she said she'd bring the food, then she's going to a movie with her friends.
W I hope you are paying for their tickets.
M Hey, that's a good idea. What a great thank-you gift!

C. Listen and fill in the blanks.

M Are you free this evening?
W No, I have to study for a math exam tonight.
M That's too bad. Well, do you need any help studying? You know that I'm really good at math.
W No, that's OK. I study better alone.
M How about going to a baseball game next week?
W That sounds like fun. I'll have plenty of time next week.
M Great. I'll check the days and times of the games.

Unit 10 In the Kitchen

KEY WORDS Track 083

Listen for these words and phrases.

burn	oven
show	mix
recipe	turn on/off
chop	boil
pasta	stir

KEY EXPRESSIONS Track 084

Listen and match each question with its correct answer.

1. Is spaghetti difficult to make?
2. Could you teach me how to make French food?
3. How long should I put this in the oven for?
4. Are these carrots small enough?
5. What's that smell?

WARM-UP Track 085

Listen and check what the speaker is making.

1. I'll put two slices of ham on this bread. I'll also add some cheese.
2. I am mixing eggs, flour, and sugar. I will put it in a round tin and bake it for 30 minutes.
3. I boil water in a big pot. Then I add some spaghetti and cook it for 8 minutes.
4. First I put some oil in the pan. Then I break one egg and drop it into the hot pan. I will fry it for about 4 minutes.
5. I'm cutting up some vegetables, putting them in a bowl, mixing them a little, and then adding some dressing.

LISTEN FOR IT Track 086

Listen and check what the speaker needs to do.

1. All these vegetables are very large. I have to cut them up.
2. Oh, no! The soup is boiling. I need to turn off the heat.
3. I can't remember how to make my grandmother's apple pie. I need a recipe.
4. I need five tomatoes for this pizza, but I only have one. I need to go to the store.
5. The bread is burning. I'd better take it out of the oven.

TRUE OR FALSE Track 087

Listen and write T for true or F for false.

1. **M** My dad is a really good cook. I like everything that he makes, but I think my favorite is his spaghetti. He makes it with a meat and tomato sauce. When I have spaghetti at my friend's house, I feel sorry for him. His parents do not make delicious food like my dad.
2. **W** I don't often use a recipe when I cook. I look at pictures of food on the internet to get ideas, but I don't use any recipes. Usually the food I make is good, but sometimes it's terrible. Last week I made beef with blueberries. I couldn't eat it!
3. **W** My husband does the cooking during the week. He works from home, but I have to go to my office every day. Sometimes our kids help him when they come home from school. He says he likes cooking, but I always cook on the weekends. I think we should share jobs around the house.

LISTENING PRACTICE Track 088

Listen and choose the correct answer.

Questions 1 and 2 refer to the following dialog.

M Is spaghetti difficult to make?
W No, it's very easy.
M Could you show me how to cook it?
W Well, do you just want to know how to cook pasta, or do you want to learn how to make a sauce as well?
M Oh, I guess I need a sauce, too.
W I think so. Give me that large pot so I can boil some water, and we can get started.
M Wait. I need to check something.
W What? Don't tell me that we don't have any spaghetti.
M That's right.
W I'll teach you another day.

Questions 3 and 4 refer to the following dialog.

W It was a great idea to make pizza together. It was fun!
M Yes. It's much better to make your own pizza because it's cheaper than buying it.
W What's that smell?
M Oh, no. I think the pizza is burning. Didn't you turn off the oven?
W No, I left it on to keep the pizza hot.

M And now it's black.
W It's fine. We can still eat it. Actually, it looks and smells really good. It's making me hungry, just looking at it.
M I think I'll have a salad instead.

Questions 5 and 6 refer to the following dialog.

W1 How long should I put this in the oven for?
W2 Twenty minutes should be long enough. Make that twenty-five.
W1 Have you made this recipe before?
W2 Many times. OK, so while that is in the oven, we need to make the sauce. Can you chop some carrots?
W1 Sure. Are these carrots small enough?
W2 No, you need to chop them into tiny pieces… Yes, that's better. Then, I'd like you to put them in that pan. I'm going to add some onions, then you can stir everything.
W1 Ok, sounds good.

DICTATION 1 Track 089

A. Listen and fill in the blanks.

1. All these vegetables are very large. I have to cut them up.
2. Oh, no! The soup is boiling. I need to turn off the heat.
3. I can't remember how to make my grandmother's apple pie. I need a recipe.
4. I need five tomatoes for this pizza, but I only have one. I need to go to the store.
5. The bread is burning. I'd better take it out of the oven.

B. Listen and fill in the blanks.

M Is spaghetti difficult to make?
W No, it's very easy.
M Could you show me how to cook it?
W Well, do you just want to know how to cook pasta, or do you want to learn how to make a sauce as well?
M Oh, I guess I need a sauce, too.
W I think so. Give me that large pot so I can boil some water, and we can get started.
M Wait. I need to check something.
W What? Don't tell me that we don't have any spaghetti.
M That's right.
W I'll teach you another day.

C. Listen and fill in the blanks.

W It was a great idea to make pizza together. It was fun!
M Yes. It's much better to make your own pizza because it's cheaper than buying it.
W What's that smell?
M Oh, no. I think the pizza is burning. Didn't you turn off the oven?
W No, I left it on to keep the pizza hot.
M And now it's black.
W It's fine. We can still eat it. Actually, it looks and smells really good. It's making me hungry, just looking at it.
M I think I'll have a salad instead.

LISTENING TEST Track 090

Listen and choose the correct answer.

Questions 1 and 2 refer to the following dialog.

W Pierre, you're from France, aren't you?
M Yes, I grew up near Paris.
W Could you teach me how to make French food?
M Of course. I'll teach you my favorite dish. I love cooking. It will be fun to teach you. I hope you like beef, because my favorite dish is a beef stew.
W Oh, yes. I like beef a lot. Is this a difficult dish?
M Not at all. You chop the meat and vegetables, put them in a pot with some water and salt, stir it all, and then boil.
W That sounds very easy.

Questions 3 and 4 refer to the following dialog.

M Mom, do you want me to stir this soup?
W Yes, please. That would be very helpful. I don't want it to burn.
M OK. It doesn't smell very good. What's in it?
W What do you mean it doesn't smell good? You like this soup. It's my chicken soup.
M Oh, but it looks different today.
W Well, that's probably because I didn't put the chicken in yet.
M Don't you put the chicken in first?
W No, not first. When did you become the cooking expert?
M I saw a cooking program on TV. The man put in the chicken first.

Questions 5 and 6 refer to the following talk.

W I don't like to watch cooking shows on TV. TV chefs and cooks say things like "You don't need to buy anything special to make this dish." But they always use a spice or vegetable that I don't have. They say, "This will take 20 minutes to make." But it takes me an hour. They say, "This dish looks beautiful." But it looks terrible when I make it. Cooking shows don't tell the truth. Cooking is difficult and messy. I think I'll order a pizza tonight.

DICTATION 2 Track 091

A. Listen and fill in the blanks.

W Pierre, you're from France, aren't you?
M Yes, I grew up near Paris.
W Could you teach me how to make French food?
M Of course. I'll teach you my favorite dish. I love cooking. It will be fun to teach you. I hope you like beef, because my favorite dish is a beef stew.
W Oh, yes. I like beef a lot. Is this a difficult dish?
M Not at all. You chop the meat and vegetables, put them in a pot with some water and salt, stir it all, and then boil.
W That sounds very easy.

B. Listen and fill in the blanks.

M Mom, do you want me to stir this soup?
W Yes, please. That would be very helpful. I don't want it to burn.
M OK. It doesn't smell very good. What's in it?
W What do you mean it doesn't smell good? You like this soup. It's my chicken soup.
M Oh, but it looks different today.
W Well, that's probably because I didn't put the chicken in yet.
M Don't you put the chicken in first?
W No, not first. When did you become the cooking expert?
M I saw a cooking program on TV. The man put in the chicken first.

C. Listen and fill in the blanks.

I don't like to watch cooking shows on TV. TV chefs and cooks say things like "You don't need to buy anything special to make this dish." But they always use a spice or vegetable that I don't have. They say, "This will take 20 minutes to make." But it takes me an hour. They say, "This dish looks beautiful." But it looks terrible when I make it. Cooking shows don't tell the truth. Cooking is difficult and messy. I think I'll order a pizza tonight.

Unit 11 What's Wrong?

KEY WORDS Track 092

Listen for these words and phrases.

cough	cold
headache	sore throat
fever	bruise
medicine	scratch
food poisoning	injection

KEY EXPRESSIONS Track 093

Listen and match each question with its correct answer.

1. Do you get enough sleep?
2. What's wrong with you?
3. Have you ever stayed in the hospital?
4. Are you taking any medicine?
5. How did you get that bruise?

WARM-UP Track 094

Listen and check what is wrong with the speaker.

1. I can't talk at all because my throat hurts so much.
2. My hand really hurts. I dropped a knife and cut myself while I was cooking.
3. I have a sore throat, headache, and I keep sneezing.
4. I think I need to drink more water. My head is killing me.
5. I drank some milk, and now I have a stomachache. I think the milk was too old.

LISTEN FOR IT Track 095

Listen and check why the speaker went to the hospital.

1. My daughter had her first child yesterday. Now I'm a grandmother. I went to see the baby this morning!
2. I had a small car accident yesterday and now my head really hurts.
3. I'm going to travel in Africa this summer and I needed to get some injections first.
4. fell out of a tree in our yard. I have a big bruise on my head, so Dad thinks I should see a doctor.
5. My cat scratched me, and now my whole arm is hot and red.

TRUE OR FALSE Track 096

Listen and write T for true or F for false.

1. **W** Do you get a cold every winter? Do you have a

cough right now? If you do, you need Winston's cough medicine. Just one spoonful in the morning and another spoonful at night is all you need. Its lemon taste is great for the kids, too. At only $7.99 a bottle you can't go wrong. Try Winston's today.

2. **M** Recently, I have been feeling ill. I went to see my doctor. I thought he would give me some medicine. But he said I didn't need any. He said I need to eat healthy food. He said I eat too many candies and too much chocolate. He also said I need to do more exercise. I know he's right. It's just difficult.
3. **W** My sister Vickie is in the hospital. She had a very high fever, and her body was very red. The doctors are taking care of her now. She is only five years old. I am going to visit her after school today. I'm very worried about her, but I know the doctors will help her. They say she can probably come home at the end of the week.

LISTENING PRACTICE Track 097

Listen and choose the correct answer.

Questions 1 and 2 refer to the following dialog.

W Hello, Mr. Anderson. What seems to be the trouble?
M I'm so tired all the time.
W Do you get enough sleep?
M Not really. I have trouble falling asleep.
W When did this start?
M About a month ago.
W Are you worried about anything?
M Well, I lost my job, and now I am unemployed. I am very worried about finding a new job.
W I'm sorry to hear that. I suggest doing yoga to relax before you go to bed.

Questions 3 and 4 refer to the following dialog.

M Have you ever stayed in the hospital, Tina?
W No, I've always been very healthy. How about you?
M Once. When I was twelve years old, I spent five days in the hospital.
W Five days? What happened?
M I fell down the stairs in our house and I broke my leg.
W Did it hurt a lot?
M Probably, but I don't remember much about it. All I remember is that I didn't have to go to school and my parents let me eat candy and watch movies!
W And your leg is fine now?
M Oh, yes. I have two strong legs now.

Questions 5 and 6 refer to the following dialog.

W What's wrong with you?
M I have a cold. And I have a cough. I think I have a fever as well.
W A lot of people have colds these days.
M I know. Did I say that I also have a sore throat?
W Do you want me to go to the pharmacy for you? I can get you some medicine.
M That would be great. I really do feel unwell.
W OK, well, I'll leave in about five minutes. Is there anything else that you need?
M No, just some cold medicine. Thanks, Lizzie.

DICTATION 1 Track 098

A. Listen and fill in the blanks.

1. **W** My daughter had her first child yesterday. Now I'm a grandmother. I went to see the baby this morning!
2. **M** I had a small car accident yesterday, and now my head really hurts.
3. **W** I'm going to travel in Africa this summer and I needed to get some injections first.
4. **M** I fell out of a tree in our yard. I have a big bruise on my head, so Dad thinks I should see a doctor.
5. **W** My cat scratched me, and now my whole arm is hot and red.

B. Listen and fill in the blanks.

W Hello, Mr. Anderson. What seems to be the trouble?
M I'm so tired all the time.
W Do you get enough sleep?
M Not really. I have trouble falling asleep.
W When did this start?
M About a month ago.
W Are you worried about anything?
M Well, I lost my job, and now I am unemployed. I am very worried about finding a new job.
W I'm sorry to hear that. I suggest doing yoga to relax before you go to bed.

C. Listen and fill in the blanks.

M Have you ever stayed in the hospital, Tina?
W No, I've always been very healthy. How about you?

M Once. When I was twelve years old, I spent five days in the hospital.
W Five days? What happened?
M I fell down the stairs in our house and I broke my leg.
W Did it hurt a lot?
M Probably, but I don't remember much about it. All I remember is that I didn't have to go to school and my parents let me eat candy and watch movies!
W And your leg is fine now?
M Oh, yes. I have two strong legs now.

LISTENING TEST Track 099

Listen and choose the correct answer.

Questions 1 and 2 refer to the following dialog.

W Can I leave work a little early today? I have a doctor's appointment.
M Yes, that's fine. I hope everything is OK.
W Oh, I'm not sick. I need to get a couple of injections.
M Why is that?
W I'm going to travel in some countries where I could get a serious disease. The injections will help keep me healthy.
M Which countries will you visit?
W Well, first I'll go to Kenya, then I'll go to Malawi.
M That sounds like an interesting trip. I hope the injections don't hurt too much.

Questions 3 and 4 refer to the following dialog.

M Are you OK? You don't look so good. Are you sick?
W My head hurts.
M How did you get that bruise?
W I fell off my bike and hit my head.
M I think you should see a doctor.
W No, I'm OK.
M Are you taking any medicine?
W Yes, I took some a couple of hours ago.
M Did it help stop the pain?
W Not really. Maybe I will see the doctor after all.

Questions 5 and 6 refer to the following dialog.

W I have a stomachache.
M Did you eat something strange?
W No, I had bread with jam for breakfast. I ate an apple. Oh, but I had fish for lunch and it tasted very strange.
M Maybe you have food poisoning.
W It did taste a bit funny. But I don't really like fish, so I thought it was normal.
M Well, drink lots of water. Don't eat anything else today.
W No problem. I'm not at all hungry anyway.

DICTATION 2 Track 100

A. Listen and fill in the blanks.

W Can I leave work a little early today? I have a doctor's appointment.
M Yes, that's fine. I hope everything is OK.
W Oh, I'm not sick. I need to get a couple of injections.
M Why is that?
W I'm going to travel in some countries where I could get a serious disease. The injections will help keep me healthy.
M Which countries will you visit?
W Well, first I'll go to Kenya, then I'll go to Malawi.
M That sounds like an interesting trip. I hope the injections don't hurt too much.

B. Listen and fill in the blanks.

M Are you OK? You don't look so good. Are you sick?
W My head hurts.
M How did you get that bruise?
W I fell off my bike and hit my head.
M I think you should see a doctor.
W No, I'm OK.
M Are you taking any medicine?
W Yes, I took some a couple of hours ago.
M Did it help stop the pain?
W Not really. Maybe I will see the doctor after all.

C. Listen and fill in the blanks.

W I have a stomachache.
M Did you eat something strange?
W No, I had bread with jam for breakfast. I ate an apple. Oh, but I had fish for lunch, and it tasted very strange.
M Maybe you have food poisoning.
W It did taste a bit funny. But I don't really like fish, so I thought it was normal.
M Well, drink lots of water. Don't eat anything else today.
W No problem. I'm not at all hungry anyway.

Unit 12 Recycle!

KEY WORDS Track 101

Listen for these words and phrases.

reuse	recycle
trash can	waste
save	glass
plastic	Earth
separate	can

KEY EXPRESSIONS Track 102

Listen and match each question with its correct answer.

1. Do you need a bag?
2. Do you recycle paper?
3. Can I put this glass bottle in the trash can?
4. Why is it important to recycle?
5. What's this box made of?

WARM-UP Track 103

Listen and check what the speaker needs to recycle.

1. I have lots of old newspapers to recycle now.
2. Mmm. That tomato soup was good, but now I need to wash and recycle the can.
3. I bought a new glass water bottle, so I have to recycle my old plastic bottle.
4. I never buy plastic bottles of soda, but I have a lot of empty cans.
5. I really should recycle all these old plastic bags.

LISTEN FOR IT Track 104

Listen and check what the speaker never buys.

1. I live alone and I don't like to waste food, so I never buy large bags of vegetables.
2. Plastic is not healthy, so I never buy drinks in plastic bottles.
3. I don't buy new clothes for my baby. I buy used clothes, then I will give them to another family when he gets older.
4. I don't buy paper to wrap birthday presents. I wrap them in newspaper!
5. I never buy plastic toys for my children. In fact, I make a lot of toys myself.

TRUE OR FALSE Track 105

Listen and write T for true or F for false.

1. **W** I always take my own bags to the supermarket. Some supermarkets will sell you a plastic bag for 10 cents. Other supermarkets only sell paper bags. I think paper bags are better than plastic. But it's better to reuse your own bag.
2. **M** Recycling is important. But it's better to reduce. What do I mean? Well, if I buy a newspaper every day, I have to recycle seven newspapers every week. So I only buy a newspaper on weekends. It means I reduce the amount of paper that needs to be recycled!
3. **W** My mom says I have to separate trash. But I hate it. I have to put glass in a green box. I have to put paper in a blue box, and I have to put plastic in a yellow box. Sometimes I forget and I put things in the wrong box. Then my mom gets mad and yells at me.

LISTENING PRACTICE Track 106

Listen and choose the correct answer.

Questions 1 and 2 refer to the following dialog.

W Dad, where can I put these newspapers?
M You can put them in the trash can.
W Dad! I can't just throw them away.
M Oh sorry. I wasn't listening properly. Why don't you put them in the recycling container? That's where paper should go.
W Because it's full. There is no room.
M OK, then put them on the floor next to the container. I'll take them to the recycling center later.

Questions 3 and 4 refer to the following dialog.

W What's this box made of?
M It looks like plastic to me.
W Yes, I was thinking the same thing. Do you think I can recycle it?
M Does it have any symbols on it? Often there is a symbol that tells you if something can be recycled.
W Good idea. I'll check… OK, it says PET and it has a number 1 in a triangle. What does that mean?
M We have a sign on the wall. Let's have a look.
W Right. Good news. This one is fine for recycling. That's useful information. I will try to remember those letters and the number.

Questions 5 and 6 refer to the following dialog.

M Do you need a bag, ma'am?
W No, thanks. I brought my own. Actually, I have two bags.

M Thank you for bringing a bag.
W Oh, I always bring a bag. I keep several in my car so I never forget one.
M That's a good idea. I often forget to bring my shopping bag. Or, I bring one bag, but I buy too much food, then I have to buy a paper bag as well.
W Yes, you need to plan carefully, but it is not too difficult if you are careful.
M I guess not. I think I just get hungry when I'm shopping at the supermarket so I buy too much food!

DICTATION 1 Track 107

A. Listen and fill in the blanks.

1. I live alone and I don't like to waste food, so I never buy large bags of vegetables.
2. Plastic is not healthy, so I never buy drinks in plastic bottles.
3. I don't buy new clothes for my baby. I buy used clothes, then I will give them to another family when he gets older.
4. I don't buy paper to wrap birthday presents. I wrap them in newspaper!
5. I never buy plastic toys for my children. In fact, I make a lot of toys myself.

B. Listen and fill in the blanks.

W Dad, where can I put these newspapers?
M You can put them in the trash can.
W Dad! I can't just throw them away.
M Oh, sorry. I wasn't listening properly. Why don't you put them in the recycling container? That's where paper should go.
W Because it's full. There is no room.
M OK, then put them on the floor next to the container. I'll take them to the recycling center later.

C. Listen and fill in the blanks.

W What's this box made of?
M It looks like plastic to me.
W Yes, I was thinking the same thing. Do you think I can recycle it?
M Does it have any symbols on it? Often there is a symbol that tells you if something can be recycled.
W Good idea. I'll check… OK, it says PET, and it has a number 1 in a triangle. What does that mean?
M We have a sign on the wall. Let's have a look.
W Right. Good news. This one is fine for recycling. That's useful information. I will try to remember those letters and the number.

LISTENING TEST Track 108

Listen and choose the correct answer.

Questions 1 and 2 refer to the following dialog.

M Can I put this glass bottle in the trash can?
W No, you need to separate the trash. Everyone who lives in the apartment building has to separate their trash first.
M But no one will know if I don't.
W But you want to live on Earth, don't you? You know it's important to recycle. Help save Earth!
M OK, I'll get a box for glass bottles to keep in my kitchen.
W You'd better get boxes for paper, cans, and plastic as well. They all need to be separated.
M But my apartment is too small.
W Then you need to make less trash!

Questions 3 and 4 refer to the following dialog.

W Do you recycle paper?
M Of course. And I try to buy recycled paper whenever I can. How about you?
W Yeah, me too. I saw something online about things people do with old paper. It was cool to see different ways to reuse paper.
M What kinds of things?
W I saw a bowl made of old paper and gift bags made of magazine pages.
M Oh, I've seen paper beads. You make the paper into a little ball, then paint it. You can make a necklace.
W That sounds like a fun thing to do. I might try that with my sister.

Questions 5 and 6 refer to the following dialog.

M Mom, I have a question. Why is it important to recycle?
W It's a good way to reduce waste.
M What happens if we don't recycle?
W Well, where do you think all the trash goes?
M A truck takes it away. But I don't know where the truck goes.
W It goes to a landfill—that's a place where trash is put into the ground. And it stays there, well, forever.
M It just stays there?

W Yes. Forever. It's bad for Earth, it smells bad, and it looks bad.

M Yuck. That makes me feel sad. I don't want to make any trash.

DICTATION 2 Track 109

A. Listen and fill in the blanks.

M Can I put this glass bottle in the trash can?

W No, you need to separate the trash. Everyone who lives in the apartment building has to separate their trash first.

M But no one will know if I don't.

W But you want to live on Earth, don't you? You know it's important to recycle. Help save Earth!

M OK, I'll get a box for glass bottles to keep in my kitchen.

W You'd better get boxes for paper, cans, and plastic as well. They all need to be separated.

M But my apartment is too small.

W Then you need to make less trash.

B. Listen and fill in the blanks.

W Do you recycle paper?

M Of course. And I try to buy recycled paper whenever I can. How about you?

W Yeah, me too. I saw something online about things people do with old paper. It was cool to see different ways to reuse paper.

M What kinds of things?

W I saw a bowl made of old paper and gift bags made of magazine pages.

M Oh, I've seen paper beads. You make the paper into a little ball, then paint it. You can make a necklace.

W That sounds like a fun thing to do. I might try that with my sister.

C. Listen and fill in the blanks.

M Mom, I have a question. Why is it important to recycle?

W It's a good way to reduce waste.

M What happens if we don't recycle?

W Well, where do you think all the trash goes?

M A truck takes it away. But I don't know where the truck goes.

W It goes to a landfill – that's a place where trash is put into the ground. And it stays there, well, forever.

M It just stays there?

W Yes. Forever. It's bad for Earth, it smells bad, and it looks bad.

M Yuck. That makes me feel sad. I don't want to make any trash.

How to Use the App

EnglishCentral

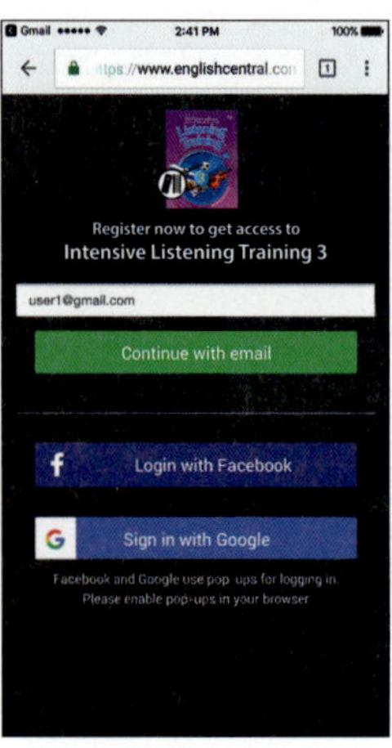

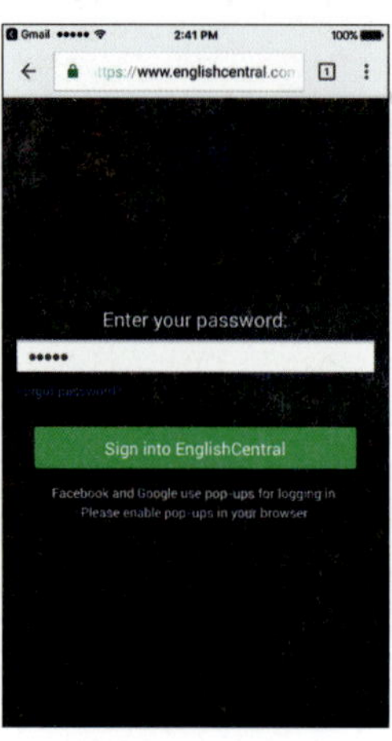

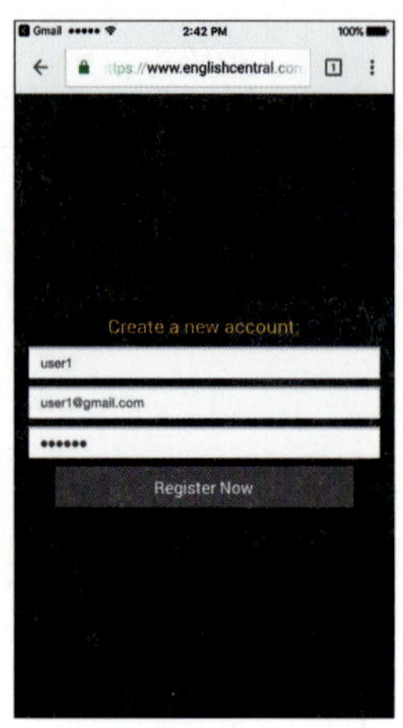

1. Scan the QR code at the back of the book.

2. Type your email address. Then click on "Continue with email."

3a. If you already have an EnglishCentral account, enter your password.

3b. If you don't have an EnglishCentral account, add your name, email, and password. Then click on "Register Now."

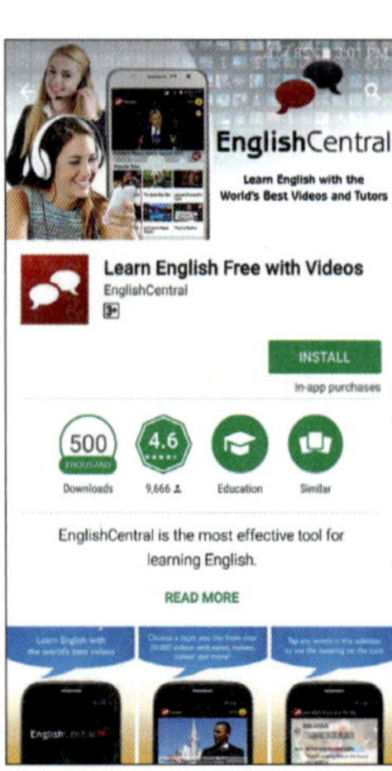

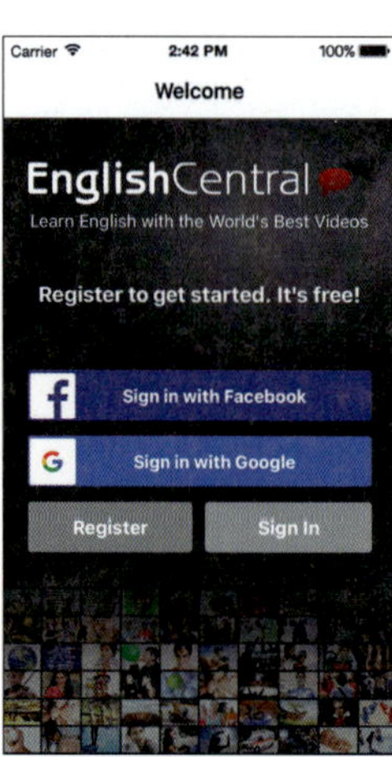

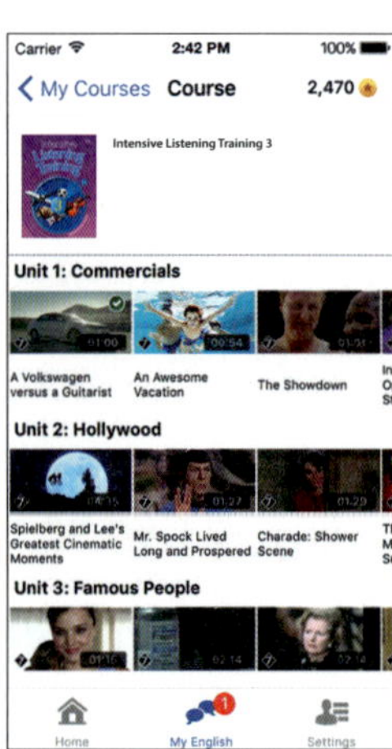

4. You now have the textbook course in your account. Click on "START."

5. Install the EnglishCentral app.

6. Click on "Sign In." Sign in with the email address that you used in #2.

7. You will see your textbook course when you log in. Complete all the units to finish the course.

David Bohlke • Anne Taylor

3

Answer Key

Intensive Listening Training

David Bohlke • Anne Taylor

Answer Key

Unit 1 At the Office

KEY EXPRESSIONS

1. (D) 2. (A) 3. (C) 4. (E) 5. (B)

WARM-UP

1. (A) 2. (B) 3. (B) 4. (A) 5. (A)

LISTEN FOR IT

1. (A) 2. (A) 3. (A) 4. (B) 5. (A)

TRUE OR FALSE

1. (A) T (B) T
2. (A) F (B) T
3. (A) T (B) T

LISTENING PRACTICE

1. (B) 2. (C) 3. (D) 4. (B) 5. (B)
6. (A)

DICTATION 1

A.

1. If you look at this, you can see that sales are up this month.
2. Thank you for coming, Miss Penney. I see that you have a lot of experience in this type of work.
3. I'd like three packs of paper and four packs of printer ink. Can you deliver them by Friday?
4. OK, it looks like everyone is here. So, the first thing to discuss is the Leeman project.
5. Which button do I press to make the size bigger?

B.

M Do you have any idea what's wrong with the printer? I can't get it to work.
W It might be out of paper.
M That's what I thought. But I checked, and there is plenty of paper.
W Is it switched off? Or perhaps there's no ink?
M That's it. The black ink has run out.
W Oh, and there isn't a spare ink in the cupboard.
M Who should I see about ordering ink?
W Marina is in charge of stationery supplies.
M Got it.

C.

W Mark, have you finished the sales report yet?
M Almost. I'll have it on your desk by the end of the day.
W Actually, You can give it to me tomorrow afternoon. I have some new details. You'll have to change a lot of the numbers for the new office building.
M Oh, no. It looks like I'll be working late tonight then.
W Yes, sorry about that. But I really appreciate your hard work.
M At least it's Friday tomorrow.

LISTENING TEST

1. (A) 2. (B) 3. (A) 4. (D) 5. (C)
6. (A)

DICTATION 2

A.

W I really enjoyed your presentation. In your workplace, do you do all the things that you described?
M In fact, I do. Since we started using the five-step process, all of our staff are much happier. And their work is better.
W Wow. I'd love to know more about how that works. I'd like to make some changes at the company where I work, but I don't really know where to start.
M Well, I'd be happy to answer any questions.
W Could I have your business card?
M Sure. It has my office number and work email address.
W Thank you.

B.

M Hello? Amy?
W Yes. Is that Patrick? You don't sound very good.
M No, I feel terrible. I'm afraid I need to use a sick day today.
W OK, well I hope you feel better tomorrow. Is there anything that needs to be done today?
M Well, if you have time. I left a pile of documents by the copier. I was going to copy them and then give the copies to everyone on the finance team. You couldn't ask Tim to do that for me, could you?
W Sure. And I'll ask him to leave the originals on your desk.
M Thank you so much.

C.

M We've run out of paper and pens again! The stationery was delivered just a couple of days ago.

W I know. It's becoming a problem. I think people are taking things home.

M I agree. I think we need to ask the staff to fill in a form each time they take an item of stationery.

W Yes. If they have to sign a form, they will be less likely to take extra things.

M OK, well, I will mention it at the next meeting. I'm sure plenty of people will complain, but I think it's necessary.

W Great. Well, I support you in this decision.

Unit 2 On Time

KEY EXPRESSIONS

1. (D) 2. (C) 3. (A) 4. (E) 5. (B)

WARM-UP

1. (B) 2. (B) 3. (A) 4. (A) 5. (A)

LISTEN FOR IT

1. (B) 2. (A) 3. (B) 4. (A) 5. (A)

TRUE OR FALSE

1. (A) T (B) F
2. (A) F (B) T
3. (A) T (B) F

LISTENING PRACTICE

1. (D) 2. (D) 3. (C) 4. (C) 5. (A)
6. (B)

DICTATION 1

A.

1. School starts at 9:00, but it takes 45 minutes to get there by bus. I need to be at the bus stop at 8:05 if I want to get to school on time.
2. According to the train schedule, the last train to Baker Street leaves at 11:45. It's already 11:35, so I'll have to run!
3. It's my parents' 20th wedding anniversary. I have to be at their house by 3:30 to decorate their house for a surprise party!
4. I have an interview for an office job at 11:00. I have to arrive twenty minutes before the time of the interview.
5. My mom shouted at me for coming home late after school last night, so I have to be home by 5:00 every day from now on.

B.

M Look at the time! It's already a quarter to one.

W Really? How time flies. It's almost time to get back to the office. Why does lunch time always go by so quickly?

M I know. I'd better hurry and finish my lunch. I think I'll get a doggy bag for the rest of this spaghetti. It's too good to leave.

W We got here at twelve, but it seems like only a few minutes.

M I know. Let's call the waitress and get the check.

W Put your wallet away. It's my treat. It is your birthday after all!

C.

M How much longer until we land in Singapore?

W About six and a half hours.

M That's still so long. I'm getting bored now.

W You'll just have to read your book or watch another movie. I'm going to try to get some sleep. And besides, the pilot said that we will arrive ahead of schedule.

M I guess that's a good thing.

W Well, it's a lot better than arriving behind schedule. Last time I traveled by airplane, we left two hours late!

LISTENING TEST

1. (B) 2. (A) 3. (A) 4. (B) 5. (C)
6. (D)

DICTATION 2

A.

M What time do you begin work?

W I start work at 10:30 every morning. I like that I don't start very early.

M How late do you usually work?

W 6:00. On Fridays I sometimes work until 8:00 because the store stays open later.

M Do you ever work on Saturday?

W Yes, I sometimes put in a half day.

M What's your busiest month?

W December. It's because of the Christmas season. While everyone is out shopping, I'm working hard!

B.

W Aren't we going to the neighborhood meeting tonight? It's almost time to leave. Why are you making popcorn?
M No, they postponed the meeting until next week.
W Oh, so when is the meeting now?
M It's not until next Thursday at 7:00.
W How long have you known that?
M Brian phoned me a few hours ago to let me know.
W I really wish you had told me ahead of time. It's really annoying. I hurried home from work. I could have finished my reports instead.
M I'm sorry. I'll mark it on the calendar so we don't forget.

C.

M I'd like to see Dr. Wilson, please.
W Do you have an appointment?
M My appointment was at 3:30.
W It's nearly 5:00, sir. The doctor is with his last patient of the day.
M I know, but I got stuck in traffic. Can I see him first thing in the morning?
W Hmm. Let me see… Yes, he has an opening at 8:30 tomorrow. But if you miss that appointment too, we will have to charge you a fee.

Unit 3 Feeling Good

KEY EXPRESSIONS

1. (E) 2. (A) 3. (D) 4. (B) 5. (C)

WARM-UP

1. (B) 2. (A) 3. (B) 4. (A) 5. (B)

LISTEN FOR IT

1. (A) 2. (A) 3. (B) 4. (A) 5. (A)

TRUE OR FALSE

1. (A) T (B) F
2. (A) F (B) T
3. (A) T (B) T

LISTENING PRACTICE

1. (B) 2. (D) 3. (A) 4. (C) 5. (B)
6. (D)

DICTATION 1

A.

1. We have to do a big homework assignment, but I didn't understand the instructions that the teacher gave us.
2. My boss wants me to stay late and finish a report, but I promised my wife that we would go to the movies.
3. My grandmother is sick again. She is ninety-five, so I don't think she will get better this time.
4. My parents agreed to buy me a car. It's amazing news!
5. Yesterday, my sister took my favorite shirt without asking. I'm still mad at her.

B.

M Are you angry at me? You seem upset.
W I'm not mad, I'm just disappointed.
M Why? What did I do?
W You were supposed to come to the movie theater yesterday afternoon. I waited for an hour, but you never showed up. I tried to call and text you, but you didn't answer your phone.
M Oh no! I'm so sorry. Please don't be annoyed. I forgot all about that. I dropped my phone, and I had to go with my mom to get it repaired. Then she wanted to get ice cream.
W I guess that's a good excuse. But I really wanted to see that movie.

C.

W How's your job going these days, David?
M It's OK, I guess…Actually, it's not great.
W What's wrong?
M I'm sick and tired of working six days a week.
W You knew that the hours were long when you took the job.
M I know. But I didn't know how frustrated it would make me feel. Whenever my friends or family make plans for the weekend, I can't go.
W But you have Sundays off.
M I know, but my friends usually want to do stuff on Saturdays.

LISTENING TEST

1. (B) 2. (C) 3. (A) 4. (B) 5. (D)
6. (D)

DICTATION 2

A.

W I feel miserable.
M Why? What's wrong?
W Well, do you ever feel frustrated?
M Yes, especially when I study hard for a test but get a bad grade.
W Exactly. I worked really hard for my biology test, but when I looked at the questions, I couldn't remember anything.
M You probably did better than you think.
W No, I already got my result. I failed.
M Then you need to talk to your teacher. Maybe she can give you some advice on how to study more efficiently.
W I guess. I'm just embarrassed to talk to her when I got such a bad score.
M No, I'm sure she'll be happy to help you.

B.

W Bill, you got 100% on this test.
M Did I really? I'm really surprised!
W Yes, I am very surprised as well. I have to ask you something, Bill. Did you copy your answers from Sam's test? You were sitting next to him, and your answers are almost the same as his.
M Um, well, yes. I'm afraid I did, Miss Parker. I didn't have time to study for the test.
W Oh,(B)ill! You're smart enough to pass this test without cheating.
M I'm sorry, Miss Parker. I've never cheated before, and I feel very bad.

C.

M When do you get nervous, Karen?
W Nervous? I suppose when I have to speak in front of a group of people.
M Me too. I have to give a presentation in class next week and I really don't want to.
W I'm glad I don't have to do that. But my teacher gave me some good advice last year. She said I should practice my presentation in front of a mirror.
M Talk to myself in front of a mirror? That sounds crazy!
W No, it really helps. Practice talking, and time how long it takes. It will make you feel less nervous, and it will help you make sure your presentation is the right length.
M Hmm, maybe I'll try that.

Unit 4 I Love It!

KEY EXPRESSIONS

1. (C) 2. (B) 3. (A) 4. (E) 5. (D)

WARM-UP

1. (B) 2. (B) 3. (A) 4. (B) 5. (B)

LISTEN FOR IT

1. (B) 2. (A) 3. (B) 4. (B) 5. (A)

TRUE OR FALSE

1. (A) F (B) T
2. (A) T (B) T
3. (A) T (B) T

LISTENING PRACTICE

1. (C) 2. (B) 3. (D) 4. (A) 5. (B)
6. (C)

DICTATION 1

A.

1. The best way to spend a rainy day is to sit on the sofa and read a great book.
2. A lot of my friends hate math, but I love to study math. It's more interesting than reading.
3. It makes me very happy when I help other people. Because of this, I'm thinking about becoming a nurse.
4. My favorite place to go is the beach. I can swim in the sea, which is much better than a pool.
5. I always get up early because it makes me feel full of energy. I love watching the sun rise.

B.

M Mary, do you like reading?
W Oh yes, I love to read.
M Do you read a lot of novels?
W Not really. I only read nonfiction because I prefer to learn something new while I am reading. And to be honest, I read more magazines than books.
M Which magazines do you like?

W I'm crazy about fashion magazines and nature magazines. I love to read about interesting animals. How about you? Do you read a lot?
M I don't read magazines, but I do like to read detective stories.

C.

What is something that annoys you? I can't stand rude people. For example, I hate people who try to push in front when I am waiting in line. Please wait! I also hate people who use their phone when they are waiting at a traffic light. The light goes green, and their car doesn't move. They are too busy looking at their phone, and they don't see the light change. It's rude behavior! Stop looking at your phone, everyone! Oh, and don't use your phone when you are at the movie theater. It's annoying to see the light from your phone when I am trying to watch the movie.

LISTENING TEST

1. (B) 2. (B) 3. (A) 4. (C) 5. (D)
6. (C)

DICTATION 2

A.

M How did you like that book I lent you?
W It was awful. I don't know why you gave it to me.
M You think so? I thought it was wonderful. What didn't you like about it?
W Well, for one thing, it was so long. I prefer reading short stories. And I didn't like the main character, Ruby. She was very rude and unfriendly. I wasn't interested in finding out what happened to her.
M I'm sorry that you didn't like it. I was going to recommend another book, but maybe that's not a good idea.
W I usually like the books you suggest, so go ahead.

B.

W Do you have any hobbies?
M I'm into photography these days.
W That sounds like an expensive hobby.
M Not really. I mean, the camera was a little expensive, but I didn't buy a fancy one. You don't need to buy the best camera to take good photos.
W Do you print out your photos?
M No, I look at them on my computer, or I share them with my friends online. I think it's a waste of paper to print out lots of pictures.
W Yeah. And that would be expensive as well.

C.

M Would you like to do something tonight?
W I don't feel like going out. Can we just hang out at home?
M Sure. Let's watch a movie.
W A movie sounds good. I downloaded a couple of movies the other day. Why don't we watch one of those?
M As long as they're not too serious. I'd like to watch something fun.
W Not a problem. They are both comedies. I heard that they are both really funny, so I think you'll like them both.
M Great. Let's watch them both.

Unit 5 Working Life

KEY EXPRESSIONS

1. (D) 2. (C) 3. (E) 4. (A) 5. (B)

WARM-UP

1. (A) 2. (B) 3. (B) 4. (A) 5. (A)

LISTEN FOR IT

1. (B) 2. (A) 3. (B) 4. (A) 5. (B)

TRUE OR FALSE

1. (A) T (B) F
2. (A) F (B) F
3. (A) F (B) T

LISTENING PRACTICE

1. (B) 2. (B) 3. (C) 4. (D) 5. (B)
6. (D)

DICTATION 1

A.

1. I love reading, so it would be great to be around books all day.
2. I've always been good at growing flowers and plants. I also enjoy being outdoors.
3. My best subjects in school are math and science,

especially biology. I also like helping people, so I want to work in a hospital.

4. I don't want to work in an office or sell things. I think I'd be good at fixing things.
5. My dream is to design school buildings. Most schools are ugly, so I want to make beautiful schools where everyone wants to study.

B.

M Who do you work for?
W I work for(A)BC Technology. I've been there for about four years.
M What do you do exactly?
W I sell new products to stores in three different cities. We develop computer accessories, so it's my job to persuade stores to stock our products.
M Do you enjoy it?
W Yes, I get to meet a lot of people, and I have to visit a lot of stores every day, so I don't spend the day sitting at a desk. It's fun to explain our new products to other people.
M That sounds like an interesting job.

C.

My father recently got a promotion at work. He works really hard, so we are all proud of him. He moved from assistant manager to executive manager at the architect's office where he works. He got a pay increase of 5%, and he is now in charge of more people. He also gets a company car now. He used to supervise 15 people, but now he is in charge of 30 people. He has a lot more work to do. He seems to work longer hours now, and I think he has a bit more stress, but I'm sure he will get used to it.

LISTENING TEST

1. (A) 2. (D) 3. (A) 4. (D) 5. (C) 6. (B)

DICTATION 2

A.

W OK, Mr. Smith. Well, you seem to be generally healthy, but your heart is a little fast. Is your job stressful?
M Only when I have a big project to complete. I'm a plumber, and most of my jobs are small. But I work for myself, not an employer, so it's sometimes difficult to take a break or a vacation.
W How many hours do you work without a break?
M Most days I work from 8:00 a.m. until 6:00 p.m., but if the job is difficult, I might have to work until as late as 10:00 at night.
W I see. Well, I think you need to start taking some more breaks, for your health.

B.

M How long have you been with your company, Daniella?
W For about six months.
M How do you like it so far?
W It's going well. I'm really glad that I studied business studies. It is really helping me to be a good business person.
M How much vacation time do you get?
W I get ten paid days off a year, but that will increase to twelve after two years, and fifteen days after three.
M Do you get any benefits?
W There is a company pension, and I can get a discount on a gym membership. And there is free breakfast in the staff break room.

C.

M Long time no see, Liz.
W Felix! It's great to see you. I heard that you opened a gardening business.
M That's right. I love gardening, so I thought I might as well get paid to do it. So now I have my own company. There are three of us working as gardeners.
W Nice. I work for Johnson Dental Clinic—the one on 3rd Street.
M Oh really? Are you a dental assistant?
W Actually, I'm a dentist.
M Oh, well done! That's great. You always were the smart one in the class!

Unit 6 School Life

KEY EXPRESSIONS

1. (E) 2. (D) 3. (A) 4. (C) 5. (B)

WARM-UP

1. (B) 2. (A) 3. (A) 4. (B) 5. (A)

LISTEN FOR IT

1. (B) 2. (B) 3. (B) 4. (A) 5. (B)

TRUE OR FALSE

1. (A) T (B) F
2. (A) T (B) T
3. (A) F (B) T

LISTENING PRACTICE

1. (B) 2. (C) 3. (B) 4. (D) 5. (A)
6. (C)

DICTATION 1

A.

1. I wasn't good at P.E. or science, but I really enjoyed social studies when I was a student.
2. The only class I was good at in school was math, but English was my favorite.
3. I liked chemistry the most in high school because I liked doing experiments.
4. I was never a very good student, but I did enjoy history. I had a great teacher.
5. I used to like classes where I could make something. That's why I enjoyed art so much.

B.

W What year are you in?
M I'm a senior.
W In college?
M No, I'm still in high school, but I'm going to college next year.
W Do you know what you will study in college?
M I hope to go to medical school eventually, so I plan to get a bachelor's degree in chemistry first. I'll also take a lot of math and biology classes, of course.
W It sounds like you have planned out your future well.
M I hope so, but I know that I have a lot of work to do if I want to succeed.
W Well, good luck, Simon.

C.

I have a big exam tomorrow. It's for my social studies class. I find the class a bit boring, so I didn't really study much. Now I have to cram for the exam tonight. My teachers all say that it's bad to cram for an exam. I think they are probably right because I forget everything that I learned right after the exam. Maybe I would remember more if I studied more carefully over several weeks. Anyway, it's too late now! Wish me luck, because I'm going to need it! It's OK if I get a C. I just don't want to fail.

LISTENING TEST

1. (B) 2. (D) 3. (C) 4. (A) 5. (A)
6. (C)

DICTATION 2

A.

W How many classes are you taking?
M I'm taking three this time. I was going to take French but decided against it.
W Are you taking chemistry? I was hoping we could be study partners.
M Yes, I'm taking chemistry, history, and a math class.
W OK, I'm taking chemistry and French. Have you taken French?
M No, but I took Korean last year. It was really cool to learn a new way of writing.
W That sounds really difficult. French is hard enough for me, and that uses the same alphabet as English!

B.

M Hey Miranda! Did you get into medical school?
W Yes, I start in the fall.
M Wow, that's great. You must be so excited.
W Yeah, but now I'm worrying about the tuition fees.
M But you knew it was expensive when you applied.
W Yes, I did, but I didn't really think that I would be accepted. So now I have to borrow a lot of money to pay for my tuition.
M But that's normal for medical students. All your classmates will have to do the same. It's fine. You'll make lots of money after you graduate.

C.

M Have you finished the math homework, Sonya?
W Not quite, but I'm almost done.
M Can you help me with a couple of the problems? I don't understand how to do them.
W Sure. Hey, what grade did you get on the last test?
M I got a B, but I really wanted an A.
W I can help you study for the next test if you like. I'm doing really well in this class.
M That would be great.
W Let's get something to eat, then go to the

library for a while?
M Sure. It's hard to study when I'm hungry!

Unit 7 A New Home

KEY EXPRESSIONS

1. (D) 2. (C) 3. (E) 4. (B) 5. (A)

WARM-UP

1. (B) 2. (A) 3. (B) 4. (B) 5. (A)

LISTEN FOR IT

1. (B) 2. (A) 3. (B) 4. (A) 5. (B)

TRUE OR FALSE

1. (A) T (B) F
2. (A) T (B) F
3. (A) F (B) T

LISTENING PRACTICE

1. (C) 2. (D) 3. (B) 4. (A) 5. (C)
6. (B)

DICTATION 1

A.

1. Do you like the new sink and counter? It's so much more fun to cook now!
2. I bought new furniture to celebrate my new job. My new sofa and armchairs are very comfortable.
3. Thanks to my new bed, I finally sleep well at night.
4. My kids are lucky because they have a room where they can store and play with all their toys.
5. The shower and sink are both new. The window gives the room lots of light.

B.

W Have you finished redecorating your bedroom?
M Almost, but there are still a few things to do. The store already delivered the bed and drawers. But we still need to paint the walls.
W What color are you painting them?
M Actually, it's hard to decide. I think blue would be good, but my wife wants to paint them green.
W Why don't you paint three walls one color, and paint the last wall the other color? It's popular these days.
M That's an interesting idea.
W Plus, blue and green look good together. It'll look nice.

C.

W So this is a townhouse?
M Yes, I love it because I have a great view from the top floor.
W But you have to go upstairs and down again several times a day.
M It's fine for me.
W There are too many stairs for me. It seems very tiring. Have you met your neighbors?
M Yes, we went and introduced ourselves when we first moved in. They seem nice.
W You should invite them to dinner.
M We probably will.

LISTENING TEST

1. (B) 2. (A) 3. (D) 4. (B) 5. (C)
6. (C)

DICTATION 2

A.

W Do you live in the city, Tom?
M No, I recently moved to the suburbs.
W I sometimes think about moving to the suburbs. I have a studio apartment in the city center.
M I used to rent an apartment downtown, but I wanted more space. I have a dog, so an apartment wasn't good for him.
W So where do you live?
M I have a house on Freeport Road, near the library.
W That's a nice area. I sometimes go for walks in that neighborhood.
M Yes, it's very quiet, and there is a nice park with tennis courts near my house.

B.

M What do you do for a living, Soo Kyung?
W I'm a realtor. I help people buy and sell houses.
M What do you like most about your job?
W I like looking inside other people's houses. It's very interesting. It gives me lots of ideas for decorating my own home.
M But I'm sure you see some ugly houses, too.
W I do, and I hate visiting houses that don't have air conditioning in the summer. But most of the time, I really enjoy my job.

M It sounds interesting.

C.

M Come in. Dinner's almost ready.
W I'm sorry I'm late. I had some trouble finding your house.
M Yes, the streets can be a little confusing around here.
W How many rooms do you have?
M Four. The kitchen is through that door, and my bedroom's over there.
W Where's the bathroom?
M In there. Why don't you have a seat?
W OK. Your sofa looks comfortable.

Unit 8 Places to Go

KEY EXPRESSIONS

1. (B) 2. (E) 3. (D) 4. (A) 5. (C)

WARM-UP

1. (A) 2. (A) 3. (B) 4. (A) 5. (B)

LISTEN FOR IT

1. (A) 2. (B) 3. (B) 4. (A) 5. (A)

TRUE OR FALSE

1. (A) T (B) T
2. (A) F (B) T
3. (A) F (B) F

LISTENING PRACTICE

1. (D) 2. (B) 3. (A) 4. (C) 5. (B)
6. (D)

DICTATION 1

A.

1. I spent two weeks on a cruise ship last summer. I stopped in Spain, Portugal, Italy, and France.
2. I recently got a job in Thailand, so I spent my last vacation in Cambodia because it is near there.
3. I don't like traveling because I don't like hotels, so I stayed at home last year.
4. My holiday in New York and Boston was so much fun last winter, even though it was cold.
5. I went to visit my aunt who lives in China a couple of months ago. It was great.

B.

W Hello. Giselle's Travel.
M I'd like to confirm a flight, please.
W Can I have your name and flight number?
M Yes, it's Jonathon Fielding, Flight 755.
W OK, you're confirmed, Mr. Fielding, on Flight 755 for this Friday morning. Please note that the departure time has changed.
M Oh really?
W Yes, the flight now leaves London Heathrow at 8:30 instead of 8:00. You will arrive in Seoul thirty minutes later than originally scheduled.
M That's even better! I can sleep a little longer on Friday.

C.

M Have you ever been abroad?
W Yes. I went to Europe last year.
M How was it? What cities did you visit?
W I flew to Paris, then I took a train to Milan and Rome. It was amazing.
M Didn't you visit London? I've always wanted to go there.
W No, I didn't have enough time, but I did go through Switzerland on the train. The view of the mountains was beautiful.
M I'd really like to visit another country someday. I need to save up enough money first.

LISTENING TEST

1. (B) 2. (B) 3. (A) 4. (C) 5. (D)
6. (D)

DICTATION 2

A.

M Oh, look, Ji-Min! There's a sign for the beach resort. And here is the resort.
W It's smaller than I expected. It looked much bigger in the pictures that travel agent showed us.
M It looks fine to me. Why don't you wait here in the hotel lobby while I check in?
W No, I'll come with you. They'll probably need to see my passport, and I have a few questions.
M I hope you aren't going to complain about anything.
W No, of course not. I want to ask about breakfast. I can't remember if it is included in the price or not.
M I think it's included, but you can ask.

B.

M Good evening, ma'am. May I see your boarding pass and passport?
W Here you are. I have my children's passports as well. For my son and my daughter.
M Thank you. Where are you traveling from?
W We flew in from Chicago. We're going on a cruise.
M I see. How long will you be here in London?
W Just one night. Our cruise leaves tomorrow.
M And can you give me the address of the hotel where you are staying tonight?
W Yes. It's Hotel Windsor, Chancery Lane.

C.

W Hello, I have a reservation under the name Samantha Baker.
M Ah, yes, Miss Baker. You are staying with us for three nights.
W That's right.
M I see you booked a non-smoking room with an ocean view. A single room. That all looks good. You are in room 712, which is on the 7th floor.
W Great. What time should I check out?
M Checkout is at 11 a.m.

Unit 9 Plans and Appointments

KEY EXPRESSIONS

1. (D) 2. (A) 3. (B) 4. (E) 5. (C)

WARM-UP

1. (B) 2. (A) 3 (B) 4. (A) 5. (A)

LISTEN FOR IT

1. (B) 2. (A) 3. (B) 4. (A) 5. (A)

TRUE OR FALSE

1. (A) T (B) T
2. (A) F (B) T
3. (A) T (B) T

LISTENING PRACTICE

1. (A) 2. (A) 3. (D) 4. (B) 5. (A)
6. (A)

DICTATION 1

A.

1. I was going to play computer games at my friend's house, but my mom says I have to visit my grandmother.
2. I arranged a soccer game with my friends, but it is pouring rain, so we can't play.
3. I planned to go to a movie with my sister, but I have a terrible headache.
4. I arranged to take today off, but my boss wants me to finish an urgent report instead.
5. I lost my wallet, so I can't pay for my train ticket to the beach. I'll have to stay at home.

B.

W Hi, Mike. What's up? I'm calling to see if you want to watch a movie or something.
M Hi, Susan. I'm just getting ready to go out.
W Do you have a date tonight?
M Yes. I'm going to a concert withBlake. Remember? We're going to see Allie Felix at the Downtown Arena.
W Oh, right. That's tonight? Well, I'd better let you finish getting ready.
M Yeah, I'm running a little late.
W OK. Give me a call tomorrow, and we can make plans for next week. I hope you have a good time tonight.

C.

I wish it were the summer vacation already. But I have school for two more weeks. I have a math exam on Tuesday, an English exam on Wednesday, and a chemistry exam the week after. But I can't study much this weekend because it's my mom's birthday and she wants the whole family to go on a big picnic. It will be fun, but I really need to study. I think I will do well on my English exam, but I'm not very good at math and chemistry.

LISTENING TEST

1. (C) 2. (B) 3. (D) 4. (B) 5. (A)
6. (C)

DICTATION 2

A.

W Are you coming to the picnic tomorrow?
M I'll try to go. But I'm not sure yet if I can make it.
W Why's that?

M I have church until 11:00.
W That's not a problem. It doesn't really start until noon.
M In that case, I think I can go.
W Come anytime. It'll go until 5:00.
M Should I bring something to eat or drink?
W No, just bring yourself!

B.

W Hi, Joe. I'm excited about your party tomorrow. What time should I come?
M Come to my apartment any time after 6:00.
W Sounds good. Have you arranged food for the party?
M Yes, my mom and her friends are going to cook.
W That's nice of them. Is your mom coming to the party?
M No, she said she'd bring the food, then she's going to a movie with her friends.
W I hope you are paying for their tickets.
M Hey, that's a good idea. What a great thank you gift!

C.

M Are you free this evening?
W No, I have to study for a math exam tonight.
M That's too bad. Well, do you need any help studying? You know that I'm really good at math.
W No, that's OK. I study better alone.
M How about going to a baseball game next week?
W That sounds like fun. I'll have plenty of time next week.
M Great. I'll check the days and times of the games.

Unit 10 In the Kitchen

KEY EXPRESSIONS

1. (D) 2. (E) 3. (B) 4. (A) 5. (C)

WARM-UP

1. (A) 2. (B) 3. (A) 4. (B) 5. (B)

LISTEN FOR IT

1. (A) 2. (B) 3. (B) 4. (A) 5. (B)

TRUE OR FALSE

1. (A) F (B) T
2. (A) F (B) F
3. (A) F (B) T

LISTENING PRACTICE

1. (A) 2. (B) 3. (C) 4. (B) 5. (C)
6. (D)

DICTATION 1

A.

1. All these vegetables are very large. I have to cut them up.
2. Oh, no! The soup is boiling. I need to turn off the heat.
3. I can't remember how to make my grandmother's apple pie. I need a recipe.
4. I need five tomatoes for this pizza, but I only have one. I need to go to the store.
5. The bread is burning. I'd better take it out of the oven.

B.

M Is spaghetti difficult to make?
W No, it's very easy.
M Could you show me how to cook it?
W Well, do you just want to know how to cook pasta, or do you want to learn how to make a sauce as well?
M Oh, I guess I need a sauce, too.
W I think so. Give me that large pot so I can boil some water, and we can get started.
M Wait. I need to check something.
W What? Don't tell me that we don't have any spaghetti.
M That's right.
W I'll teach you another day.

C.

W It was a great idea to make pizza together. It was fun!
M Yes. It's much better to make your own pizza because it's cheaper than buying it.
W What's that smell?
M Oh, no. I think the pizza is burning. Didn't you turn off the oven?
W No, I left it on to keep the pizza hot.
M And now it's black.
W It's fine. We can still eat it. Actually, it looks and

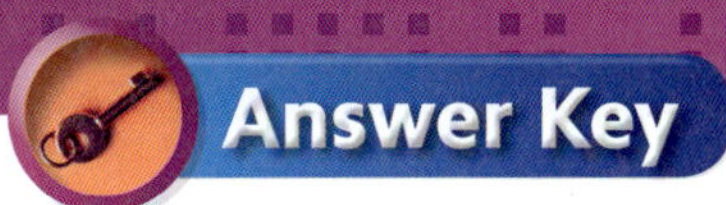

smells really good. It's making me hungry, just looking at it.

M I think I'll have a salad instead.

LISTENING TEST

1. (A) 2. (A) 3. (B) 4. (B) 5. (C)
6. (D)

DICTATION 2

A.

W Pierre, you're from France, aren't you?
M Yes, I grew up near Paris.
W Could you teach me how to make French food?
M Of course. I'll teach you my favorite dish. I love cooking. It will be fun to teach you. I hope you like beef, because my favorite dish is a beef stew.
W Oh, yes. I like beef a lot. Is this a difficult dish?
M Not at all. You chop the meat and vegetables, put them in a pot with some water and salt, stir it all, and then boil.
W That sounds very easy.

B.

M Mom, do you want me to stir this soup?
W Yes, please. That would be very helpful. I don't want it to burn.
M OK. It doesn't smell very good. What's in it?
W What do you mean it doesn't smell good? You like this soup. It's my chicken soup.
M Oh, but it looks different today.
W Well, that's probably because I didn't put the chicken in yet.
M Don't you put the chicken in first?
W No, not first. When did you become the cooking expert?
M I saw a cooking program on TV. The man put in the chicken first.

C.

I don't like to watch cooking shows on TV. TV chefs and cooks say things like "You don't need to buy anything special to make this dish." But they always use a spice or vegetable that I don't have. They say, "This will take 20 minutes to make." But it takes me an hour. They say, "This dish looks beautiful." But it looks terrible when I make it. Cooking shows don't tell the truth. Cooking is difficult and messy. I think I'll order a pizza tonight.

Unit 11 What's Wrong?

KEY EXPRESSIONS

1. (D) 2. (A) 3. (B) 4. (E) 5. (C)

WARM-UP

1. (B) 2. (A) 3. (A) 4. (A) 5. (A)

LISTEN FOR IT

1. (B) 2. (B) 3. (A) 4. (A) 5. (B)

TRUE OR FALSE

1. (A) T (B) T
2. (A) F (B) F
3. (A) F (B) T

LISTENING PRACTICE

1. (C) 2. (D) 3. (B) 4. (C) 5. (A)
6. (B)

DICTATION 1

A.

1. My daughter had her first child yesterday. Now I'm a grandmother. I went to see the baby this morning!
2. I had a small car accident yesterday, and now my head really hurts.
3. I'm going to travel in Africa this summer and I needed to get some injections first.
4. I fell out of a tree in our yard. I have a big bruise on my head, so Dad thinks I should see a doctor.
5. My cat scratched me, and now my whole arm is hot and red.

B.

W Hello, Mr. Anderson. What seems to be the trouble?
M I'm so tired all the time.
W Do you get enough sleep?
M Not really. I have trouble falling asleep.
W When did this start?
M About a month ago.
W Are you worried about anything?
M Well, I lost my job, and now I am unemployed. I am very worried about finding a new job.
W I'm sorry to hear that. I suggest doing yoga to relax before you go to bed.

C.

M Have you ever stayed in the hospital, Tina?
W No, I've always been very healthy. How about you?
M Once. When I was twelve years old, I spent five days in the hospital.
W Five days? What happened?
M I fell down the stairs in our house and I broke my leg.
W Did it hurt a lot?
M Probably, but I don't remember much about it. All I remember is that I didn't have to go to school and my parents let me eat candy and watch movies!
W And your leg is fine now?
M Oh, yes. I have two strong legs now.

LISTENING TEST

1. (A) 2. (C) 3. (B) 4. (D) 5. (D)
6. (C)

DICTATION 2

A.

W Can I leave work a little early today? I have a doctor's appointment.
M Yes, that's fine. I hope everything is OK.
W Oh, I'm not sick. I need to get a couple of injections.
M Why is that?
W I'm going to travel in some countries where I could get a serious disease. The injections will help keep me healthy.
M Which countries will you visit?
W Well, first I'll go to Kenya, then I'll go to Malawi.
M That sounds like an interesting trip. I hope the injections don't hurt too much.

B.

M Are you OK? You don't look so good. Are you sick?
W My head hurts.
M How did you get that bruise?
W I fell off my bike and hit my head.
M I think you should see a doctor.
W No, I'm OK.
M Are you taking any medicine?
W Yes, I took some a couple of hours ago.
M Did it help stop the pain?
W Not really. Maybe I will see the doctor after all.

C.

W I have a stomachache.
M Did you eat something strange?
W No, I had bread with jam for breakfast. I ate an apple. Oh, but I had fish for lunch, and it tasted very strange.
M Maybe you have food poisoning.
W It did taste a bit funny. But I don't really like fish, so I thought it was normal.
M Well, drink lots of water. Don't eat anything else today.
W No problem. I'm not at all hungry anyway.

Unit 12 Recycle!

KEY EXPRESSIONS

1. (D) 2. (C) 3. (A) 4. (B) 5. (E)

WARM-UP

1. (B) 2. (B) 3. A) 4. (B) 5. (B)

LISTEN FOR IT

1. (B) 2. (B) 3. (A) 4. (B) 5. (A)

TRUE OR FALSE

1. (A) T (B) T
2. (A) F (B) T
3. (A) T (B) F

LISTENING PRACTICE

1. (B) 2. (C) 3. (D) 4. (B) 5. (B)
6. (A)

DICTATION 1

A.

1. I live alone and I don't like to waste food, so I never buy large bags of vegetables.
2. Plastic is not healthy, so I never buy drinks in plastic bottles.
3. I don't buy new clothes for my baby. I buy used clothes, then I will give them to another family when he gets older.
4. I don't buy paper to wrap birthday presents. I wrap them in newspaper!
5. I never buy plastic toys for my children. In fact, I make a lot of toys myself.

B.

W Dad, where can I put these newspapers?
M You can put them in the trash can.
W Dad! I can't just throw them away.
M Oh, sorry. I wasn't listening properly. Why don't you put them in the recycling container? That's where paper should go.
W Because it's full. There is no room.
M OK, then put them on the floor next to the container. I'll take them to the recycling center later.

C.

W What's this box made of?
M It looks like plastic to me.
W Yes, I was thinking the same thing. Do you think I can recycle it?
M Does it have any symbols on it? Often there is a symbol that tells you if something can be recycled.
W Good idea. I'll check… OK, it says PET, and it has a number 1 in a triangle. What does that mean?
M We have a sign on the wall. Let's have a look.
W Right. Good news. This one is fine for recycling. That's useful information. I will try to remember those letters and the number.

LISTENING TEST

1. (A) 2. (D) 3 .(A) 4. (B) 5. (A) 6. (C)

DICTATION 2

A.

M Can I put this glass bottle in the trash can?
W No, you need to separate the trash. Everyone who lives in the apartment building has to separate their trash first.
M But no one will know if I don't.
W But you want to live on Earth, don't you? You know it's important to recycle. Help save Earth!
M OK, I'll get a box for glass bottles to keep in my kitchen.
W You'd better get boxes for paper, cans, and plastic as well. They all need to be separated.
M But my apartment is too small.
W Then you need to make less trash!

B.

W Do you recycle paper?
M Of course. And I try to buy recycled paper whenever I can. How about you?
W Yeah, me too. I saw something online about things people do with old paper. It was cool to see different ways to reuse paper.
M What kinds of things?
W I saw a bowl made of old paper, and gift bags made of magazine pages.
M Oh, I've seen paper beads. You make the paper into a little ball, then paint it. You can make a necklace.
W That sounds like a fun thing to do. I might try that with my sister.

C.

M Mom, I have a question. Why is it important to recycle?
W It's a good way to reduce waste.
M What happens if we don't recycle?
W Well, where do you think all the trash goes?
M A truck takes it away. But I don't know where the truck goes.
W It goes to a landfill – that's a place where trash is put into the ground. And it stays there, well, forever.
M It just stays there?
W Yes. Forever. It's bad for Earth, it smells bad, and it looks bad.
M Yuck. That makes me feel sad. I don't want to make any trash.